ERRATA

Two aerial photos were cropped in the attempt to show the desired building and unfortunately resulted in an oversight and an error:

- **PAGE 41.** The photo caption should read:

  Case Hall was built in 1961 employing lift slab technology. (All the floor slabs were poured on top of each other, and then, one at a time, the floors were jacked up the columns and welded in place. Ballyhooed as the construction technique for all future buildings, however, it was only used this once at MSU.) Case Hall was the first "Living/Learning" undergraduate dormitory and the first coed dormitory.

- **PAGE 61.** Jenison Fieldhouse is pictured rather than Munn Ice Arena. Interestingly, Ted Simon worked on the Jenison Fieldhouse construction project as an employee of Christman Construction Company when he was also a student at MSC.

A Rendezvous
with MSU

A Rendezvous with MSU

Ron Flinn

MICHIGN STATE UNIVERSITY PRESS | EAST LANSING

MICHIGAN STATE
U N I V E R S I T Y

Printed and bound in the United States of America.

☉ The paper used in this publication meets the minimum requirements
of ANSI/NISO Z39.48-1992 (R 1997) (Permanence of Paper).

ISBN: 978-0-9967252-5-5 (cloth)

20 19 18 17 16 15 14   1 2 3 4 5 6 7 8 9 10

Designed and typeset by Charlie Sharp, Sharp Des!gns, East Lansing, MI

*This book is dedicated
to my wife, Norene,
who made it all possible.*

CONTENTS

ACKNOWLEDGMENTS

'd be remiss if I didn't acknowledge MSU's being accessible and affordable in 1957. (All the engineering schools in New York State were private and expensive.)

Norene's willingness to join me in pursuing my dream—which required both of us to quit good jobs, move 500 miles away from our relatives, and assume we'd have no problem finding new jobs—required significant faith and a bit of naiveté.

The wonderful staff of the Building and Utilities department, the Physical Plant division, and now the Infrastructure Planning and Facilities (IPF) division have been great colleagues and friends, as well as supporters as I moved through various assignments.

Over the years as I've responded to "Why did you do it that way?" or "How was that decision made?" with answers that, many times, included quotes from campus notables, I would be told, "You need to write a book." In recent years, two individuals who frequently encouraged/pestered me were Lynda Boomer and Gus Gosselin.

As I entered retirement, Dan Bollman agreed it was important that the history of MSU's facilities organization be documented. He was kind enough to provide an office and computer access. Deborah Dohm was close by, and she frequently provided assistance and guidance on how to use Microsoft Word.

In discussing my challenge with Communications Director for Infrastructure Planning and Facilities Michelle Lavra, she strongly suggested we bring an experienced writer/editor onto the team. She introduced me to Robert Bittner, a freelance author and magazine writer, who agreed to participate. Michelle's advice and Bob's involvement as editor have been essential in transforming my memories, notes, and drafts into a smooth-flowing story.

As I was completing my manuscript, I greeted Douglas Noverr, Professor Emeritus, one day as I was approaching the North Campus Parking Ramp, and he inquired if I was making progress my book. He also informed me that he was attending a book signing, later that week, as his book *The Rise of a Research University and the New Millennium, 1970–2005* (also known as the third and last MSU Sesquicentennial Book) was recently published. His subsequent encouragement, and advice on how to access campus photos, has proven to be of great value.

As forecasted by Doug Noverr, Whitney Miller at University Archives ably assisted in locating the historic pictures used in this book. The current campus pictures are courtesy of the MSU Communications and Brand Strategy team, Kevin Epling, and photographers Greg Kohuth, Kurt Stepnitz, and Derrick Turner. Derrick also took additional pictures of athletic facilities, where needed. Francie Todd in the College of Engineering, Stephanie Perentesis at the MSU Libraries, and Portia Vescio with University Archives assisted in the pursuit of other photos.

Jeff Kacos, Lorena Griffin, Jade Freeman, Kendra Schroeder, Katie Gervasi, Scott Friend, Christopher Perry, Nicholas Voss, Jill Tuley, Connie Jordan, and Todd Wilson in MSU's Infrastructure Planning and Facilities were of great assistance in finding and developing maps and other illustrations. Bob Nestle, Bob Ellerhorst and Scott Gardner in IPF, confirmed various dates and statistics.

A Rendezvous
with MSU

Olds Hall of Engineering, with an insert of Agnes McCann, the "Engineer's Friend."

PROLOGUE

I arrived at Olds Hall, on the campus of Michigan State University, along with my friend Bob Able on a cold April day in 1957. We were two community-college graduates from upstate New York on a mission to learn how much credit we would receive for our two-year Associate of Applied Science degrees in construction technology toward a BS in civil engineering.

As we were introducing ourselves to the young lady at the counter, an older woman came out of a nearby office and said, "I need to see you two fellows back here.

We learned later that her name was Agnes McCann. She was officially the dean's secretary but actually functioned as an associate dean. She told us that she was on a blue ribbon committee to determine the curriculum of the two-year colleges being developed in Michigan. A major question was whether the schools should grant two-year associate degrees or fully transferable college-credit courses. Since we had recently graduated from a two-year program, she wanted our opinion.

We pointed out that most of our classmates seemed happy with their two-year degree, but a few of us wanted to obtain a four-year degree. I said it would be great if the schools could offer both.

The advice of two unknown students may or may not have been useful in the final decision making. What made this experience remarkable for me was that someone who looked like my grandmother—a woman who raised me from the time I was two years old—and held a powerful university position had bothered to ask a couple of 19-year-olds what she should do.

That so impressed us that Bob and I decided MSU was the place for us. We cancelled plans to visit the other large Midwestern campus we were considering, the University of Illinois in Champaign-Urbana.

That decision set the course for my life.

A decade earlier I had never even heard of Michigan State. My first knowledge of the school was obtained from a *Life* magazine article in the early 1950s that featured a picture of the undefeated 1952 Michigan State College football team, recognized as national champions that year.

I was impressed. But I remember thinking, *East Lansing, Michigan? That's way out west. I wonder if I will ever see it.*

1.

Getting Prepared

M y roots go back to central New York. I was born on a dairy farm, in Madison County, on August 6, 1937. It was in a very rural area, without running water or electricity, but it was within the shadow of Colgate University, five miles away. That gave me a very early focus on wanting to go to college, even though no one in my family ever had or wanted to.

My mother, Jennie Marie (always just "Marie" to the family), died when I was two. The cause was *phlegmasia cerulea dolens*, a rare form of deep vein thrombosis that can be triggered by pregnancy. Back then, they called it "milk leg" or "white leg," due to the stark white appearance that accompanied the loss of circulation in the legs. Following her death, I, my older brother Bob, and my younger sister Marie Isabell—who was a preemie, so small she was fed with an eye dropper—were all taken in by my maternal grandparents, Walter and Isabell Harvey. They literally took on a whole second family. There were already 12 other people living in the two houses on what was known as the Soule farm, including their own teenage children. Her second daughter, Theo, was thrust into being a major assistant in handling the large household.

My grandmother was the "chief cook and bottle washer." I remember that she was spared from doing laundry by hand, however; her Maytag washing machine had a kick starter for the gas engine!

Once we were settled, my father, Hugh, left to find work in Ithaca. (My mother had completed high school, but he had only an eighth-grade education.) He learned welding in Ithaca. Then he met a girl from Scotland—he had emigrated from Scotland himself as a young boy—and he remarried.

After World War II broke out, my grandfather Walter was able to obtain a job with a rifle manufacturer, which enabled my grandparents and us kids to move to the small hamlet of Eaton, New York, about three miles away from the Soule farm.

Our father would visit us regularly, though. He always had good clothes, drove a new car. He made sure we had new Schwinn bicycles. We even had a pony with a cart and a saddle: Tony the Pony. How many kids have a pony with a cart? After the war, things got tougher for him. But the one thing I admired about my father was that he could bounce back the next day after losing everything.

Bob was the most heavily impacted by our mother's death because he was old enough to remember her and know that she was missing. He would run through the house screaming for her. I think that's why he wound up always being the withdrawn and negative one in the family. I was the positive one.

When I say "withdrawn," I mean Bob was really bashful. It was so bad that when it was time for him to start first grade—there was no kindergarten at our school—my grandmother convinced the teachers to let me go with him because he was so shy. Now, Bob was a year older than I was, so I ended up starting first grade when I was five years old. My brother sat alone in the corner while I played with all of the other kids.

The school was a simple, wood-frame structure with first and second grade taught in the same room. For Halloween, our masks were paper sacks that we drew on with crayons. There was nothing like bus service for kids who lived outside of town, so the school hired a neighbor from two miles away to pick us up and take us to school in his own car.

As we got a little older, Bob and I would spend our summers going up to the family farm every day to help out. Our great-uncles preferred to farm like their father did around 1900. So my brother and I became experienced driving teams of Belgian horses, putting up loose hay, thrashing, participating in silo-filling bees, etc. We also learned to drive a 1935 Chevy pickup truck at a very young age. I'm convinced that growing up with the older generation (grandparents for parents and great-uncles as uncles) gave us the skills to work with and relate to an older generation.

Bob and I also shared a newspaper route for the *Syracuse Herald Journal*. We even did our own bit to aid the war effort: I recall that at one point students were issued gunny sacks and asked to pick milkweed pods to be used in the manufacture of kapok life preservers for the military. Little did I know that those early years in Eaton during World War II—when almost everything from sugar, shoes, gasoline, and tires was rationed—were training me to be frugal and conserve, skills that would prove invaluable in the years to come.

When we entered seventh grade and moved into junior high, we were bused the three miles to Morrisville, where the high school was located. We weren't alone: Morrisville-Eaton was a "central school system," and students were bused in from a number of nearby communities, including Peterboro.

Peterboro was the historical home of Gerrit Smith, who, in the 1800s, was a powerful abolitionist and pillar in the Underground Railroad, which provided slaves escaping from the South a route to Canada, where they would be free and safe. Because the area was a well-known sanctuary, once the Civil War ended, a number of black families chose to settle in Peterboro. As a result, and thanks to the busing situation, I now had black classmates for the first time. Having people of color as classmates and friends was very meaningful to me then.

During high school I worked part time in Tainter's Market in Morrisville, a ma-and-pa grocery store where I performed all duties except buying from suppliers. That meant sweeping, stocking shelves, cutting meat, clerking, and serving customers. Fortunately, electricity arrived in the late '40s. In 1953, I helped install indoor plumbing.

When I was a junior in high school, I decided I was going to go into engineering, and I received encouragement from our guidance counselor, William Behnk.

Maybe engineering sounds like an unusual choice for someone raised by farmers and who had spent so much time working on farms. But my brother and my great-uncle still liked doing things the old-fashioned way, using horses instead of machines, thrashing tools rather than combines. Bob reveled in that. At one point he asked me to consider joining him as an owner of the farm because he was sure we were going to inherit it from my great-uncle. I wasn't so convinced. (It turned out not to happen.)

I said, "If we do that, we're going to have to buy up half the county." I'd done some work with my cousins, Jack and Lloyd Newton in DeRuyter, which was about 20 miles away, and they were going at it big time: combines, custom threshing and silage. It struck me that that's what you had to do if you were going to thrive. You had to go big. But Bob wanted to keep things on a small, family-run scale. I didn't think that would work.

This kind of summed up how divided our interests were. When we were having to decide what subjects to study in high school, our grandmother asked my Uncle Almott—everybody called him Bud—for his advice. Bud knew us well. He said, "Bob needs to take courses for Future Farmers of America [FFA]. And Ron should take college-entrance courses." Thank God he said that. It set the stage for me to take the math and science track, where I was fortunate to study under some high-quality teachers.

So I was already on a different path than Bob. Then, for some reason, I got focused on structures. I would hear people say something like, "You know, we really need a bridge here." So I'd think, *Okay, how big do the support members need to be? How do you do the foundations?* Of course, when you're on a farm, you're involved in this stuff all the time. My great-uncle would want to rebuild the sugar house where they made maple syrup. Or there were structures like the big chicken coop that was rotting. We had to go and help brace something up, so I looked at how you go about doing it *right*. I was very drawn to that, and just why I'm not sure. But that was the part of engineering that I always wanted to do: structures.

That's how I ended up taking college-bound classes in high school when most of my peers, including my brother, took FFA curriculum. I was also drafted to be the senior-class president (my graduating class totaled 37) and president of the student council, and was honored to attend Empire Boys State, held at Colgate University. The Boys/Girls State program was launched in the late 1930s by the American Legion as a means for promoting democratic ideals among America's youth. High schools throughout each participating state would select certain students to attend state meetings where two boys and two girls would be chosen as delegates to the annual meeting in Washington, DC. Although I didn't get chosen for the Washington delegation, that experience triggered my deep and lifelong interest in politics.

■ ■ ■

Because of my unusually early introduction to first grade as a five-year-old, I graduated from high school in 1954, when I was just 16. I knew I was college-bound, but I had absolutely no resources. I had to find a school to attend that was low cost. All the engineering schools were private and, thus, very expensive.

To me, the best alternative seemed to be to move to Buffalo, where my dad and stepmother had moved to gain employment during World War II. Their apartment had a second bedroom, and I could live with them while attending a two-year college with affordable tuition, Erie County Technical Institute (ECTI). ECTI's construction-technology program was as close to civil engineering as I could find that I could afford. So I started there in the fall of 1954. By that time, my dad had a small contracting business in Buffalo, and I ended up working with him occasionally while I was going to school, helping him remodel homes.

In addition to being affordable, Erie County Tech also had a cooperative training program. So at the tender age of seventeen, I was placed with Krehbiel & Krehbiel, in Tonawanda. It was a 20-person civil-engineering, land-surveyor outfit. It was love at first sight. I remember thinking, *This is what I am going to do for the rest of my life. Except it's going to say Flinn and Associates over the front door!* The big assignment while I was there was designing the last five miles of the New York Thruway.

I had another job as well. I worked nights at the *Courier-Express* newspaper, where I wound up being chief copyboy. The *Courier-Express* was a major daily morning paper in Buffalo with a history going all the way back to the early 1800s. Samuel Clemens—better known as Mark Twain—even worked there briefly in the mid-1800s. It no longer exists, I'm sad to say, having closed its doors in 1982. Working there was one of the best experiences I've ever had. It also played a small part in my eventually coming to study at MSU.

The newspaper was a union shop, so I was required to join the newspaper guild, affiliated with the newly formed AFL-CIO. I didn't have much fondness for unions at the start. My opinion softened when I observed two situations. The union was able to persuade management to retain a beloved but terminally ill reporter, allowing his widow to receive the full $10,000 death benefit. The union also convinced the paper to keep its part-time copy staff, made up mostly of college students like myself, rather than replace them with full-time employees.

After a few months, I became head of the copy staff, my first supervisory experience.

It was at the *Courier-Express* that I first heard how beautiful the Michigan State campus was. When a city editor heard me say I was thinking of attending MSU, he swung around in his chair and asked, "Have you been there?" I said no. Then he told me his hobby was visiting as many campuses across the country as possible. He had probably visited a hundred already. He said, "If MSU isn't the most beautiful campus in the country, it's in the top five." Obviously, I wasn't choosing schools based on beauty, but his comment stuck with me.

Of course, I was also a busy student during this time.

As I began classes at ECTI, the math teacher, Harry Panton, wrote his name on the chalkboard and added "PE" after it. He explained that the PE designation signified he was a professional engineer, licensed to practice in the state of New York. That gave me yet another goal.

The curriculum exposed us to all phases of design and construction, as well as labor relations, enhanced letter-writing skills, estimating, etc. Each day was a full eight hours with lots of drafting classes.

The professor of physics, Warren Marsh, stated at the beginning of our first class that "no one gets an 'A' in this class unless they volunteer for extra assignments." My new friend Bob Able and I decided we would do it. Professor Marsh's assignment for me was to draw a large diagram of how a gas refrigerator functioned. He was teaching Niagara-Mohawk employees at night on how to service such units.

Raymond Jones taught construction estimating and had a unique teaching style. He entered the room and announced, "Two people to each drafting board. Now go to the windows." We were on the third floor overlooking Elmwood Avenue. "See that Niagara-Mohawk substation? The drawings and specifications on your drafting boards are for that building. Your grade will be based on how close you come to estimating the winning bid, adjusted for inflation." He then walked out and never returned. Fortunately, we were told to buy the *Means Estimating Handbook,* a small, spiral-bound book that proved essential. (Today, the line of Means books fills a small bookshelf, and the third edition of the *Handbook* is nearly 1,000 pages long.)

My education wasn't limited to the classroom.

PHOTO COURTESY OF THE AUTHOR.

Bob Able and me with the model of our award-winning project. Graduating with an associate degree in Construction Technology from Erie County Technical Institute required developing complete construction drawings and specifications as well as a model of the project. Our project theme reveals my agricultural background.

As I've noted, my father emigrated from Scotland with his family. He was only eight years old, but he remained a British subject his whole life. He had a different perspective on race than many Americans at that time, and he wanted to make sure my eyes were open to the wrong of racial prejudice. One day, as we were driving to a home-remodeling job in what was known as the black district, he waved to a black couple standing in their yard. He told me the woman was a lawyer, and her husband was a professor at the University of Buffalo. But they were shut out of buying a house in Williamsville, where other faculty lived, just because they were black.

I might have thought that couple's experience was unique if I hadn't known Dave Wright.

One day I saw Dave Wright, one of two black students in our class, dressed up in a suit and tie. I asked, "What's up?" He told me he saw an ad for a sweeper job at a large corporate factory, so he called up and was told, "Come on over." Dave was a Navy veteran from Korea with a wife and child, and he needed additional income beyond what he received through the GI Bill. He was extremely articulate and handsome. And he was as black as ebony. A few hours later, I saw him again. But this time he was angry, beating in his locker door. I asked him what had happened.

"When I talked to them on the phone, I had that job," he said. "But when I walked through the door, and they saw the color of my skin . . . 'No jobs available,' they said."

Experiences like these affected me deeply, convincing me that this country was in desperate need of change.

■　■　■

As we were nearing the end of our two years at ECTI, Bob Able and I got serious about getting a BS in civil engineering, so we searched the ECTI library for information on possible schools. We came across a pamphlet from South Dakota School of Mines, which had a very low tuition rate. We decided it would be wise to ask Harry Panton what he thought.

Professor Panton said, "That might be a very fine school. But I'd suggest that you want to go to a school where the name of the school is known more than 30 miles out of town because after you graduate, you'll need a job. But first you need to get an interview with a potential employer. And maybe if they've heard of the school, they'll at least talk to you."

Given that advice, I sent off letters to Penn State, University of Michigan, Michigan State, and the University of Illinois. MSU and U of I were willing to discuss giving us credits for our two-year degrees. The other schools wouldn't. Since Michigan was closer to Buffalo than Illinois was, we decided to first visit MSU. (Ironically, I couldn't help noticing recently that a March 2, 2015, *Wall Street Journal* article mentioned South Dakota School of Mines and Technology as having the best return on investment of any public university.)

Looking back, my training at Erie County Tech was fantastic, especially in light of how it prepared me for the different situations I would confront later as a professional.

. . .

Both Bob and I needed money if we were going to continue our education. So we decided we should work for a year and build up enough income to enter a university in the fall of 1957. Bob got a job with the Corps of Engineers, working on the Seaway Project up on the St. Lawrence River. The best-paying job I could find was being a draftsman with Union Carbide's Electro-Metal-lurgical Division in Niagara Falls. While there, I was able to take night classes at Millard Fillmore College—the night school of the University of Buffalo (a private university then)—and Union Carbide paid the tuition.

I reported to Bob Lilly, a chemical engineer, and designed piping installations in various Union Carbide plants: Niagara Falls, New York; Ashtabula, Ohio; and Sault Sainte Marie, Michigan. In less than a year, I became the piping expert that everyone came to for advice.

The piping training was invaluable, but there were drawbacks to the job. The daily commute to Niagara Falls from Buffalo, in the years before expressways, taught me to never live in a large city or commute a long distance to work. In addition, the design office where I worked was located adjacent to the electric furnaces that produced acetylene. The emissions from the furnaces settled on the gable roof like snow and was removed by "avalanching" the buildup into gondola wagons drawn up alongside the building. There were several other chemical plants located there because of the low-cost, hydro-produced electricity. All these plants dumped their waste at a site that became infamous as the highly toxic "Love Canal." I was convinced I should avoid working in such an environment in the future, if possible.

During the three years I was in Buffalo, I had joined the New York National Guard Corps of Engineers. By joining, I was able to avoid having my education interrupted by being drafted. But I also learned a lot about how to take care of myself, what it takes to be an effective leader, and what encourages others to follow and support those in command positions.

In those days you did not have to attend boot camp. I was just required to attend weekly drills and spend two weeks each summer at Camp Drum (now Fort Drum) in Watertown, New York. I joined the 152nd Engineer Battalion of the 27th Armored Division. Captain Albert L. Gaines became company commander after the first year or so. Captain Gaines was an engineer, employed by Westinghouse, and was one of the best officers I have ever met.

He also happened to be yet one more black associate who made a powerful and positive impression on me.

I eventually moved up to the position of Sergeant E-5. I worked in battalion headquarters alongside majors and colonels, which gave me some great insight into leadership and decision making.

I still didn't have any money to speak of. Being a member of the National Guard, I was able to compete for expenses-paid admission to a military academy and was offered an alternate position to the newly established Air Force Academy in Colorado. By the time that offer came along, I had already made the firm commitment to come to Michigan State.

I made another, even more important commitment around that time as well.

In the summer of 1956, my high-school sweetheart, Norene Smith, moved to be near me in Buffalo. She took a room in the YWCA and worked as a secretary at Buffalo Forge Company. Clearly, she was willing to join me in pursuing my dream no matter where it might lead.

It led us to Michigan.

We were married September 14, 1957, and arrived in East Lansing less than two weeks later.

Arrival

My dad and stepmother drove Norene and me from New York to Michigan. We arrived in East Lansing in late September 1957, with classes set to start in just a few days.

Even though I had visited the MSU campus the previous summer, I still remember feeling overwhelmed at the size of the place. It was *huge*. I'd never been at a school with over 5,000 students. Michigan State had 17,000.

Married housing was tight. Beginning in 1945, the school had provided "trailer apartments" and barracks housing for married students; preexisting housing could not keep pace with the large influx of veterans following World War II. By the time I arrived, the converted trailers were gone, replaced by University Village and Cherry Lane Apartments on the South Campus. The first phase of Spartan Village had just been completed, but the waiting list was nine months long. So I had been advised, during my summer visit, to arrange housing before we moved to town. (When my friend Bob Able arrived, he moved into the recently completed Brody complex, since it was compulsory to live on campus if you were a single student who had yet to earn Junior status.) We bought an 8' × 36' house trailer in what was known as "Trailer Haven" behind Coral Gables, east of the campus on Grand River Avenue. Although we

The North Campus Power Plant where I started work as a Student Engineer in late September 1957.

PHOTO COURTESY OF MSU ARCHIVES AND HISTORICAL COLLECTIONS.

The Shaw Lane Power Plant. The Turbine Room Addition, on the East side of the building was underway as I arrived.

were some distance from the bustle of campus, it wasn't particularly peaceful: In August, a fire had seriously damaged Coral Gables and reconstruction was underway, almost at our front door.

Construction was happening on campus too.

Crews were busy building the second phase of Spartan Village as well as the Student Services building, Kresge Art Center, and additions to the Women's Intramural building (now Circle IM), Men's Intramural building (now IM West), and the Shaw Lane Power Plant to house a steam-driven electrical-generating turbine. Meanwhile, workers were putting the final touches on Erickson Hall, Van Hoosen Hall, and an expansion to the newly renamed Spartan Stadium (formerly Macklin Stadium) that added an upper tier, making it possible to accommodate 76,000 fans.

This represented a remarkable level of growth, especially since it was just two years earlier, in 1955, that Michigan State College became Michigan State

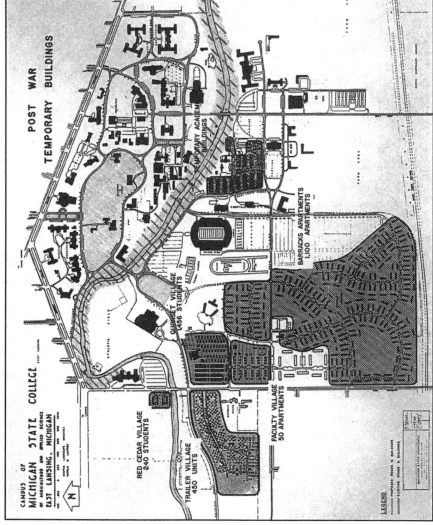

CAMPUS OF
MICHIGAN STATE COLLEGE
OF AGRICULTURE AND APPLIED SCIENCE
EAST LANSING, MICHIGAN

POST WAR
TEMPORARY BUILDINGS

A 1948 map of the MSC campus. Note how few permanent buildings existed South of the Red Cedar River and that Shaw Lane ended at Shaw Hall. By 1957, the temporary Red Cedar Village had been replaced by the Brody Complex, and Trailer Village had been replaced by University Village. Barrack Apartments, once vacated, were being removed since the permanent Spartan Village was underway. In addition, the Anthony Hall Complex and Erickson Hall were recently completed, and Men's Intermural Building (now known as IM West) was under construction.

University. Now, it was as if the school was doing everything in its power to create an expanded campus worthy of its new status.

In 1957, it had been exactly 100 years since classes began at what was first known as Michigan Agricultural College. (Officially, MSU traces its beginnings to 1855, when Governor Bingham signed a law setting aside 676 acres of woodland for the creation of a state agricultural college near the capital. The 1955 centennial yearbook described it thusly: "In the spring of 1857, the college was only a crude clearing in the wilderness of nature and the minds of men.") During those first 100 years, the school grew from a founding class of 61 students in three not-quite-finished buildings—College Hall, Saint's Rest dormitory, and a red-brick horse barn, which housed the animals students would need to work the college farm—to a world-class university of 17,000. But with the kind of enthusiastic growth I saw when I arrived, it seemed likely that only a few years would pass before the school would need to replace the temporary buildings, Quonsets, and Mead buildings with permanent classrooms and laboratories.

At that point, though, I was more focused on my immediate future. That meant classes, of course. But it also meant jobs for both me and Norene.

Fortunately, our home in Trailer Haven was next to Ann and Joe Kavanagh's place. When I learned that Joe was the assistant electrical engineer for the MSU campus, I told him I was looking for part-time employment. He found me the next day when I was registering for classes and said, "When you finish here, come over to the power plant. There may be an opening for a student employee."

The North Campus Power Plant was located at what is now the front lawn of the John A. Hannah Administration Building. There, Joe introduced me to George Karas. One of the first things Karas asked me was, "Have you ever done a piping drawing?" When I shared my Union Carbide experience, he told Adam Hulinek, who headed up the engineering office, that I should be hired. I started work the next day.

Norene had similar good luck. She was quickly hired at Flash Cleaners in the Frandor Shopping Center as the counter attendant. (At that time, Frandor was just three years old.) We did not have a car, so she walked the three miles, each way, between our trailer and the shopping center until her manager found out. He told her, "I live in Williamston. I'll pick you up in the morning and drop you off at night."

As both a student and an employee, I was able to gain an even deeper appreciation for just how vast Michigan State was compared to the other schools I'd known: Thousands of students, two power plants, two television stations (WKAR and Channel 10) enormous acreage, and new construction projects underway and in the planning stages. It was overwhelming, certainly, but it was also invigorating. Since I knew I would be here only for a couple of years, I vowed to make the most of my time on campus.

Student Years

A s soon as I started classes, I realized I would pay the price for not knowing the campus layout better. All of the classes I had selected were in buildings far apart from each other. Each morning I had to run between the Physics-Math (now Psychology) building to Jenison Fieldhouse back to Kedzie, and then to Dem Hall. My chemistry labs were in the Quonset huts and my Communication Arts classes were in one of the Mead buildings, which were World War II–era barrack-type structures (located where Wells Hall is now). And there were only 10 minutes between classes!

I spent my afternoons working out of the North Campus Power Plant. The Engineering department office was on the second floor of the office wing of the North Campus Power Plant, located southwest of Agriculture Hall (on what is now the front lawn of the John A. Hannah Administration Building).

The ground floor housed the Buildings and Utilities (B&U) administrative offices as well as the offices of the power plant manager, Jesse Campbell, and the electrical engineers, Shorty Noonon and my new friend Joe Kavanagh. There was a small conference room off the lobby, occupied by two women and a coffee pot. This was the MSU Credit Union, managed by Frances Lesnieski and one lone volunteer. While that sounds incredible today—when the MSU

Federal Credit Union is the largest university credit union in the world—just two years earlier the former credit union manager, Luther Whipple, worked half days and kept all the credit union records in his desk drawer.

The second floor housed the Engineering staff, including the newly promoted Luther Whipple, estimator, and two full-time draftsmen, Max Seeds and Don Cross. The trade shops—plumbers, electricians, etc.—were in a two-story brick building southwest of the power plant, which was shared with the University Stores department. A gambrel-roof barn, south of the trade shops, housed the Custodial department and the sheet-metal shop. I was told the telephone switchboard had been moved from the second floor of the power plant to the lower level of the museum just a year earlier.

All student employees in Engineering reported to Max Neils, who had been a member of the occupying forces in Germany at the end of World War II. His number-one assignment at MSU was inspecting all underground utility installations. Under his guidance, student employees were responsible for correcting the campus utility maps and performing site surveys. The survey crews were all students, headed up by two seniors, Bob Strong and Stan Badelt. When they graduated, I became the crew chief since I had the most training and experience in surveying. Two of our major assignments were the site surveys for the Manly Miles building and the Grounds building. (A later assignment for the student survey crew was the site survey for the proposed Bogue Street Bridge. The bridge was constructed as a City of East Lansing project.)

I rode in with Joe Kavanagh each morning. In those days, he would stop to check the work progress on a number of buildings, such as Natural Science, as they were wrapping up the campus electrical distribution conversion from 2500V to 4160V.

Ted Simon became superintendent of B&U in 1956, replacing Ed Kinney. Some months after I started working, I overheard part of a conversation in which Ted told Shorty Noonon and Adam Hulinek, "and I also don't want any 'yes men' around me!" He said it with such force that I took that statement as gospel. In the future, I made a point of always being very candid with my opinion whenever I had a conversation with Ted.

An internationally significant event occurred just after I started classes: On October 4, 1957, the Soviet Union launched the Sputnik 1 satellite. It was Earth's first orbiting satellite, and the fact that it was built by the Soviets—that

Looking East at the Temporary Academic Buildings (now the site of Wells Hall), also known as the Mead buildings, where I took my Communication Skills class, taught by Professor Marilyn Culpepper. Harold Lautner and the Site Planning Office was housed in the North Building.

our Cold War enemy beat us into space—shocked many Americans. Sputnik 1 set off the space race and increased national interest among college students in obtaining technical degrees, including engineering.

Tuition was $65 per term, but, being from out of state, I paid an additional $100 per term. After two terms, I was admitted into Upper College (College of Engineering) and was able to stop attending ROTC and taking Physical Education classes.

My advisor was Professor Leo Nothstine, who shared an office with Professor A. H. Leigh. In fact, they shared a desk! It was typical, in Olds Hall, for two faculty members to face each other across a large double desk. Because of that arrangement, it was not unusual for Prof. Leigh to chime in while I was having a discussion with Prof. Nothstine.

Before New Year's, George Karas left our department. He was selected to help Mrs. Matilda Wilson establish a branch campus of MSU at her estate, Meadowbrook Manor in Oakland County. Before becoming Mrs. Wilson, she was the widow of John Dodge of Dodge Motors. The property was his farm. For several years, the new school was known as MSU-Oakland. It is now the independent Oakland University.

Norene was moving onto a new assignment as well. After a couple of months at Flash Cleaners, she was successful in obtaining employment at East Lansing State Bank and soon became a teller. She had the opportunity to become acquainted with the campus notables, such as Ted Simon and Malcolm Trout, who banked there.

Even though Norene now had a better-paying job, it still was essential for me to work as many hours as possible. It was especially important that I work full time during the summer to have enough money for fall tuition. But just as summer term 1958 approached, the administration announced that student employees could only work 20 hours a week due to a serious budget problem. It would not be my last brush with a serious budget problem at MSU.

In those days, the State of Michigan functioned totally on a three-percent sales tax. In a typical year, that was sufficient. But 1958 was not a typical year. The entire country was experiencing what we would later call a recession. Automobile sales slumped, and Michigan was in great financial difficulty. Fortunately, I was informed that I could work full time if I was willing to help overhaul a three-megawatt turbine generator at the power plant. I jumped at the chance, becoming Kenny Green's assistant for the summer. The work was hot, dirty, and at times very physically challenging. The overhead crane for lifting heavy objects required two or more people to manually operate the chain fall; the large cast-iron turbine cover weighed several tons. On the bright side, I made many friends and gained knowledge that became invaluable in future years.

■ ■ ■

At this point, I need to mention MSU's president during my student years (and, indeed, beyond): John Hannah.

Hannah, who replaced Robert Shaw as president at MSC in 1941, became, it is safe to say, the school's most influential president to date. During his tenure, a former agricultural college became an internationally respected university with an ever-increasing student body and a reputation for both research and academics. It was Hannah's vision that brought about the greatest period of campus expansion MSU has ever seen. Of course, you cannot accomplish everything he did without rubbing some people the wrong way. But whether you were a friend or foe, you had to admit that Hannah was a man who tended to get what he wanted for Michigan State University. I will explore this more fully in Chapter 5.

During that summer of 1958, I was told that State of Michigan employees were issued scrip, as the state didn't have the currency to make payroll. However, MSU employees continued to be paid in real dollars. That is because John Hannah was able to meet with Howard Stoddard, president of Michigan National Bank, and obtain a signature loan for one million dollars to help carry us through the recession. (A few years ago, I told this story to a large group seated around a table at the dedication of the new Stadium Tower. A gentleman at the table spoke up and said my story wasn't totally accurate. He had been in the room when the transaction took place, and, he said, "There was no *signature*. There was only a handshake!")

One day, as I was leaving work and heading to class, I overheard a black gentleman ask for the boss. Ted Simon stepped out into the lobby to meet him. The visitor said, "I've got to have a job. I can't feed my family." Ted called Jesse Campbell out to the lobby and asked if he knew of any potential assignments. Jesse mentioned one. Ted said, "Put this man to work." Ted probably did not think twice about this incident; there was work to be done, so he hired somebody to do it. Yet, I knew from my past experience that not every employer saw things so clearly when the prospective employee was black. I thought, *This is a good place.* That opinion was reinforced when I learned John Hannah was cochair, with Father Hesburgh of Notre Dame, of the national Civil Rights Commission, reporting directly to President Eisenhower.

■　■　■

Married life, work, and classes kept me very busy. That doesn't mean that my friends and I didn't make time for typical college pranks.

In the late 1950s, students were not allowed to drive on campus. However, commuting students were allowed to park on a gravel lot north of the water reservoir and pumping station, a good distance south of the river. Faculty and full-time employees, though, parked in lots close to North Campus, using a special card to open the exit gates. Needless to say, all of us commuters hoped to find a way to park in those nearby lots.

Two of my fellow student employees were from Mason and frequently rode together. Tom Bergeon was a bit of a jokester, whereas Jim Ireland appeared to be somewhat gullible. One day, Tom told Jim that an erasing shield (a thin metal sheet with various openings to aid in erasing mistakes on construction drawings) would open the exit gates. We all knew this was another attempt by Tom to pull Jim's leg, and even Jim was laughing at him.

But then they each drove separately for a week or two. And one day, Tom asked Jim, "Where are you parking? I haven't seen your car lately."

"I'm parking in the faculty lot west of Shaw Hall," Jim said.

"Well, how are you getting out through the exit gate?"

"You should know," Jim said, staring at him. "I'm using an erasing shield."

Of course, Tom thought Jim was just trying to get back at him, so he admitted his previous claim was bogus and that erasing shields wouldn't work. Jim just shrugged and said, "Come with me, and I'll show you."

He did. Sure enough, it worked! We rushed back, found the box of erasing shields, and returned to the parking lot. Not a single one of the twelve shields in that box would work. Somehow, Jim had picked out the *only* erasing shield that would actually open the exit gates.

From then on, we commuters would all meet at 5:00 P.M., lining up our cars, one after another, with the first one inserting the shield to activate the gate, leaving the shield for the next, and the last one taking the shield home for the next day. (When Jim graduated, he took a job with the State of Michigan tax bureau and one day remembered all the barrack buildings that were being moved from campus to various locations in the mid-Michigan area. He investigated and discovered the contractor never paid sales tax. I was told this was the largest recovery of sales tax that year, and Jim's work was viewed as exceptional. Perhaps that made up a bit for our youthful deception.)

■　■　■

During my senior year, Norene became pregnant and, as was the rule back then, had to quit her job at the bank during her third trimester. As a result, I had to take out a National Defense Loan in order to finish college. I was easily approved since I was taking engineering classes, but the struggle to pay it off in subsequent years gave me a real understanding of the debt load many graduates carry today.

Graduation was quickly approaching, but there was still work to be done. One project in particular stands out. It did not feel so significant at the time, but it would end up setting the course for my career.

There was a serious water-pressure problem in Agriculture Hall. They had tried a booster pump to increase the pressure, but that—and other fixes—had not worked. I was asked to come up with a solution. There were two key contributors to the problem: Many fixture units had been added on the upper floors, dramatically increasing the potential for water use at any one time, and the pipes themselves had become partially blocked by lime deposits. My solution was to install a new, large riser pipe up through the building.

After the installation was complete, I visited Ag Hall with Adam Hulinek and Ted Simon to check the pressure gauge. In the past, water pressure on the fourth floor would drop to nearly zero whenever a toilet was flushed. Now, the gauge was moving gently back and forth near the maximum pressure point. My solution had worked. I do not know what course my life would have taken if it had failed. But because it succeeded, I was asked if I would be willing to stay on after graduation and work at MSU "for a year or so."

Former President Harry Truman, Governor Williams, and John Hannah at the 1960 Graduation Ceremony.

"A Year or So"

A s I approached graduation in June 1960, I was asked to stay on as a full-time employee for "a year or so." It was not a difficult choice. There were no other attractive job offers coming in, and Norene wanted to stay in East Lansing, where we had made many friends. MSU had proven itself to me as a world-class institution and a good employer. In fact, such was its reputation that former US President Harry Truman delivered the commencement address that year, which impressed both me and my father, who was a big fan of President Truman. (It was obvious that John Hannah had the ability to persuade any notable, including General Douglas MacArthur and Richard Nixon, to be a commencement speaker.)

Commencement is all about new beginnings, and we Flinns had one of our own: Our first child, Elizabeth Ann (Beth), was born on May 23. Now that we were a family of three, Norene suggested it was time to leave the trailer behind and move into a house. Fortunately, a fellow came along looking for a trailer to haul to Colorado, and we made a deal, allowing us to move into a rental house on Haslett Road.

During the late 1950s and into 1960, most proposed campus projects were envisioned as additions to existing buildings. For example, the planetarium

PHOTO COURTESY OF MSU ARCHIVES AND HISTORICAL COLLECTIONS.

A view of the North Campus Steam Tunnels, built in the early 1900s.

was an addition to the museum, and the Shaw Lane Power Plant was to be expanded to provide additional steam and electricity. However, the frequent foul odor coming from the sewage plant, immediately south and across the Red Cedar River from the Brody Complex, caused the Board of Trustees to decree in December 1959 that a new sewage disposal plant be built at a new location. Significant pressure was required to convince the East Lansing City Council to authorize replacing the old overloaded facility with a modern sewage plant on a new site requiring a large financial investment.

The in-house engineering staff designed farm buildings, such as the new sheep facility, to make way for the proposed new Engineering building to be located west of Anthony Hall. We also designed the utility extensions to new buildings: Bessey Hall, which required removal of the band shell; Owen Hall; and Case Hall all received direct buried steam and condensate return lines. I thought this was odd since similar lines installed only 15 years earlier were already in disrepair, while the steam tunnels on North Campus were 50 years old and, with minor maintenance, were in good enough condition to serve for another 50 years.

In 1959, I began helping Rene Hauser, who had graduated as a mechanical engineer and stayed on full time. He was impressed that I understood how

A view of the South Campus Steam Tunnels, built during the 1960s.

adsorption machines functioned, using steam heat to generate chilled water. (Same concept as a gas refrigerator, using heat from a natural gas flame to produce cooling.) Working with Rene is how I gained more experience in heating, ventilation, and air conditioning (HVAC). However, there was very little air conditioning on the MSU campus at that time. The watchword was "Save every dollar for an expanding campus!" That meant air conditioning was prohibited except for absolutely essential activities. For instance, it was decided that classrooms in the new Bessey Hall would be cooled for summer sessions, but the faculty office wing would not be cooled.

I recall that Dr. Henry Blosser, my nuclear physics professor, was building a model of the Cyclotron that he would build if MSU received the anticipated federal grant. He was making the model using small lead blocks and beeswax in a room on the west side of the Physics-Math building, but the afternoon sun was melting the beeswax. Rene and I tried to solve this problem by installing Koolshade screens over the windows. That did not work. So Dr. Blosser stomped over to see John Hannah and came back with authorization to install air conditioning. It was obvious: Henry Blosser was a major player!

When the decision was made to cool the library, Rene and I designed the solution in-house to keep the cost down. I designed the large basement room on the south side of the building and assisted with the HVAC design. Several years later—still mindful of every penny—I extended chilled water lines to the new Music Practice building as a low-cost cooling solution.

Early on, I attended the weekly Site Planning department staff meetings, where Harold Lautner would return from his weekly meeting with President Hannah and inform us of the latest plans. I, in turn, would then report back to Ted Simon and the rest of the B&U team. This was a fortuitous assignment; I was in on the ground floor of what was possibly going to happen, and I became friends with the entire Site Planning staff.

When John F. Kennedy became president of the United States in 1961, there was talk of the need for universities to expand rapidly to handle the Baby Boomers. In his campaign speeches, Kennedy frequently used the phrase "get this country going again" and spoke of the need to make education available to more people. With that in mind, I explored how much additional water we might need in the future to serve a rapidly growing student population. Few people were aware that MSU had two water reservoirs and pumping stations: a small one on North Campus, as part of the Power Plant complex, and the relatively new, million-gallon reservoir and pumping station on South Campus. Determining the quantity of water consumption and flow rates required a laborious, time-consuming effort to add the flow rates from each facility recorded on circular charts for each day. Many nights I took home piles of these charts and pored over them at our dining room table, tabulating the data. Norene thought I was a bit daft, but the effort paid off. In May 1961, I issued a report predicting the number of water wells we would need in order to meet the forecasted demand. Unfortunately, my graph predicted that the student population might eventually approach 40,000. That figure sounded ridiculous, apparently, and it led my superiors to conclude the report had little value. (It was very rewarding when, just two years later, the student body had already increased to the extent that the leadership was suddenly asking, "Hey, where's the report that kid wrote?")

In late 1961/early 1962, we recognized that MSU was on the verge of a major expansion. The proposed steam line from the Shaw Lane Power Plant to the new Engineering building needed to be large enough to serve the huge number of buildings that would be coming east of Farm Lane. It was decided a 20-inch steam line and a 10-inch condensate return line would be appropriate. Rene Hauser and I were able to prove that, when installing big pipes like that, a walk-through tunnel could provide an economical means for servicing them. We received approval and built the first steam tunnel on campus since the 1930s.

Rene and I also designed the first computer room on campus in association with Julian Kateley, the manager reporting to Dr. Lawrence Von Tersch in the Computer Science department. Dr. Von Tersch had overseen the development of MISTIC, the large hand-built computer housed on the fifth floor of the Electrical Engineering building and the foundation of the Computer Science program.

During this time, Ted Simon scheduled monthly evening meetings with B&U supervisors. There, a speaker, usually from our faculty, would describe their area of expertise to the group. Engineers were welcomed if they were interested, and I frequently attended. One evening in 1960, we went to the EE building and Dr. Von Tersch explained MISTIC's capabilities. When he finished, Ted asked, "Professor, do you see this technology being utilized in our business?" Von Tersch thought and thought. Then he said, "No, I really don't." Before he retired, as dean of engineering in 1988, Dr. Von Tersch was able to see just how much his computer and others had changed the world.

As we moved further into 1962, several new projects went into the design phase, including the Cyclotron and buildings for Chemistry, Biochemistry, and the Physical Plant division (formerly B&U). I was the lead structural design engineer and assistant mechanical systems design engineer for the Physical Plant building.

Up to this point, Supervising Architect Don Ross, who reported directly to John Hannah, was responsible for the design of new buildings and field inspection of all major construction projects. Sometime during 1962, Hannah issued a directive assigning Don Ross and his assistant, Bob Siefert, to Harold Lautner and assigning all field inspectors to Ted Simon. Rumor had it that the Men's IM building's poor design led to this decision. A few months after completion, the large south walls of Men's IM were tipping away from the building. I designed reinforced cantilevered concrete pilasters to prevent further movement. The "feet" are buried below the frost line, and the vertical pilasters are encased in matching brick. Very few people realize this "fix" was employed.

It was also around this time that Lisa Marie, our second daughter, was born, arriving on March 11, 1962. Soon after, Norene pointed out the need for a larger, better house.

As it happened, the Physical Plant division moved into its new building just one week before the Flinn family moved into our new home on Forest Road.

Don Cross (not to be confused with Don *Ross*) had tipped me off that the house across the street from his was empty and for sale. I was able to buy it on a land contract with a very low down payment. My home life vastly improved as Norene was elated! She at last had a home of her own. We also had good neighbors in Don and Audrey Cross. Their daughters, Felicia and Regina, were close in age to our Beth and Lisa.

When I mentioned that I had purchased a house on Forest Road at a Site Planning meeting, Harold Lautner said, "You do realize MSU is planning to acquire all that property for a research park, don't you?" I didn't, but that was good to know!

What none of us could have known—apart from John Hannah, perhaps—was that a research park would be a minor development compared with the other construction projects being dreamed of for the very near future. The next several years would see growth like no other time before or since in the history of MSU.

Build, Build, Build

The Site Planning office, reporting to Harold Lautner, was responsible for developing the Master Plan for the university with weekly input from President Hannah. Lautner would bring a large campus map—actually a very large, heavy box with a glass face, with each existing or proposed building being displayed as a scale model—to each Board of Trustees meeting.

Developing the Master Plan for the expanding South Campus, including the new Science complex, Vet Clinic, and the Fee/Akers housing complex, revealed the need for a new main east-west road and extensive utility expansion. Milt Baron, second in command in the Site Planning office, and I worked closely together on its layout, which became a boulevard with the necessary utilities placed in parallel to the road's center line. One day, as we were reviewing the design, he asked, "Could you move the steam tunnel a few feet further north and be directly under the sidewalk? That could help melt the snow and ice during the winter." We did and it worked.

The large storm and sanitary sewers needed under the road required an enormous ditch to be dug—30 feet deep and approximately 50 feet wide at the surface. After watching the backfilling operation, I said, "I'm not seeing any compaction equipment, such as sheep foot rollers, which would assure proper

Early 1960s installation of the 48-inch elliptical sanitary sewer that crosses the campus, primarily under Wilson Road. Near the Biochemistry Building, the excavation was 35 feet deep. A very large storm sewer also accompanied the sanitary sewer.

compaction." The response was, "Dozer compaction is good enough." After all construction was complete, everyone noticed that the sewer manholes had started to push up through the pavement, a sign that the backfill had not been sufficiently compacted and was still settling. I visited my former soils professor, Tony Blomquist, to determine which soil compaction specification would be best for MSU in the future, since dozer compaction clearly was *not* "good enough."

Many people today are aghast to learn that the Master Plan for the North Campus during the 1960s called for removing the small old buildings north of Ag Hall, now known as "Laboratory Row," and building a large modern structure in their place. It's obvious now that the historical significance of these buildings was not fully appreciated back then.

In the summer of 1963, I took photos to document all of the work happening on campus: the Physical Plant building under construction (B&U was renamed Physical Plant in November of that year), the Chemistry building rising from its deep basement, the Cyclotron and Biochemistry buildings' structural frames, the basement level of the first parking ramp, as well as the large storm and sanitary sewers being installed under what was to become Wilson Road. (The 48-inch elliptical sanitary sewer runs across the entire campus, from Hagadorn Road to the new sewage plant, to carry the sewage from Meridian Township as well as the campus. John Hannah did not want a sewage plant just upstream from the campus.) These facilities were some of the first to replace the temporary World War II–era Quonset huts and Mead buildings, and to address the new emerging technologies of nuclear physics, radiated-plant research, lasers, etc. All the farm facilities were moved south of Mount Hope Road to make room for this major expansion. Not surprisingly, this period gave rise to the commonly heard phrase, "The concrete never sets on John Hannah's campus!"

I had become very knowledgeable of all the existing buried utilities, designing various extensions as well structural repairs to deteriorated anchors in steam vaults. So I was often called upon to help locate utilities when the underground crew needed to excavate or repair a broken water main. It was not unusual to receive such calls for help after hours and on weekends, and I had to respond. It got to the point where it had happened so frequently during the dinner hour that Norene said, "It looks like you love MSU more than me or the kids." Of course, that was not true. But, where I came from, you took care of a decent job since another one wouldn't be just around the corner.

Today, many have forgotten the fear that prevailed in our country during this time. Our troops were already engaged in an actual war in Vietnam. But for many Americans, our Cold War with the Soviet Union was far more real and a genuine source of dread. Nuclear war was considered so probable that I, along with many other engineers and architects, became certified as a fallout shelter analyst by the Department of Defense. All new buildings were to have basement areas and other features to protect people from radiation exposure in the event of nuclear attack. Fortunately, reason prevailed and we never had to put these shelters to the test.

On a much lighter note, during this period I also developed some preliminary sketches for the first MSU Credit Union building, which was built on the south side of Trowbridge Road just west of Harrison Road.

Max Neils became a full-time inspector of building construction, leaving inspection of utility construction to me—along with the design responsibilities

A 1963 photo showing the Cyclotron exterior complete with the structural steel frame of the Biochemistry Building in the background.

for steam, water, and sewers. I also became the lead mechanical systems designer, as Rene Hauser left to become the physical plant director at Eastern Michigan University.

One of my first responsibilities in this new role was to expand our well field into the farm district to assure an adequate supply of water to campus. Increasing the well capacity would get the quantity needed to the reservoir building. But the distribution pumps at the reservoir would then need to push the water to the campus buildings—and their capacity then was the same as when they were built in 1951, which simply was not sufficient. One day, I stopped at the reservoir to check on the fluoridation system installation I had designed and spoke with Bill Emede, who was stationed there during the day to monitor the waterworks. He pointed out that the distribution pumps were struggling to keep up with the demand. I agreed that we needed to expand the capacity soon. He asked how I would do that. I recalled that Claude Erickson, who designed the original building, had shown on his drawings, in dashed lines, an addition to the south for holding additional pumps. So I said, "Probably build an addition to the south and add extra pumps."

Bill said, "Yes, every engineer who has looked at this challenge has said that."

I looked at him for a moment.

"You have something else in mind, don't you?" I asked.

He shrugged. "I'm only wondering why we don't just put in bigger pumps."

That was an excellent observation.

I rushed back to the office and pulled out the Allis-Chalmers pump catalog. Looking at the equipment available to me, I determined that if I used special elbow joints, I could install larger pumps in the very tight pump galley. I was considered a genius for developing a low-cost solution—10 percent of what a building addition would have cost! ("Save every dollar possible for an expanding campus!") But of course it hadn't been my idea at all. It came from Bill Emede, a nonengineer who happened to spend every day working with and thinking about those pumps. Bill shared his thought with me because I asked for his input. And he knew that even if it was a dumb idea, I wouldn't scoff or ridicule. You never know who will have a great idea.

■　■　■

McDonel Hall was completed in 1963 under a tight schedule and required a very long steam-tunnel extension from the Bogue Street and Wilson Road intersection east along Wilson Road and north to Shaw Lane. Few thought it would be done on time. Emery Foster, manager of Housing and Food Services, wisely scheduled a luncheon for the contractors a few weeks before the students were to arrive. It was a way of thanking them for going the extra mile to finish the work on time. It also subtly reminded them that failure was not an option. I remember overhearing W. A. Brown, the steam-pipe contractor, say, "This is the most expensive 'free' steak I've ever eaten!" He had spent substantial dollars in overtime pay to get the work done on schedule.

Here is what I remember most from that day, however: After the luncheon, President Hannah walked across the large room and introduced himself to me. (I now think he had probably been informed that I was responsible for the steam project.) This simple act caused me to realize how important it is for staff members to know that the leader knows them and cares about them. I am certain that moment meant very little to John Hannah. It was perhaps just a casual, polite gesture. Yet it made a huge impact on me and on how I work with people.

■   ■   ■

Shortly after we moved into the new Physical Plant building, a man named Vince Vandenburg stopped in to see Ted Simon. He said, "With this large construction program cranking up, you need a construction superintendent. I'm your guy." He was hired. Apparently, he came with quite a reputation.

The first time I heard Vince's name was when Luther Whipple told me about the salvage yard being separated from B&U sometime in the early 1950s. Whip (as he was known) said that when Vince came back from the war, he established a construction company. Like many people, he would visit the campus salvage yard, which was stockpiled with material and tools left over from the government-funded Public Works Administration (PWA) projects. But the manager of the salvage yard didn't like Vince—maybe because Vince was John Hannah's brother-in-law—so he billed Vandenburg Construction for some material, the same sort of material that others were allegedly taking for free. One day, when Vandenburg was at the old Administration building paying the bill, he happened to say in a loud voice, "It's too darn bad I'm the only person who has ever had to pay for anything leaving that salvage yard!" That raised some eyebrows. An investigation of the salvage yard's business practices was launched. Investigators discovered that an entire cottage had been built in northern Michigan with material appropriated from the salvage yard and with labor provided by B&U tradesmen, all of it off the books. As a result, a B&U supervisor lost his job.

Whip went on to describe the heavy interrogation the police used while interviewing the B&U staff. But, he said with a grin, "They were gentler with me since I was also the entire credit union at that time. I'm just glad they never asked me if I knew who drove the truck of salvage up to the cottage." That's because Whip himself drove the truck! He loved beer parties, and apparently there was plenty of beer to be had at the cottage site.

The second story that I heard about Vince came from Bill Emede at the reservoir. (Vandenburg Construction built the reservoir and pumping station.) Bill said that many years earlier, he and another fellow were watching the activity at Dem Hall as they were installing the concrete floor needed to convert the building into an ice arena. A Ford Model A came down the street, jumped the curb, and stopped in front of the building. A guy jumped out—hollering and yelling about the need for faster work—pulled off his

Case Hall, upper right in the photo, was built in 1961 employing lift slab technology. (All the floor slabs were poured on top of each other, and then, one at a time, the floors were jacked up the columns and welded in place. Ballyhooed as the construction technique for all future buildings, however, it was only used this once at MSU.) Case Hall was the first "Living/Learning" undergraduate dormitory and the first Co-Ed dormitory. Wilson Hall, lower center in photo, was next in '62 followed by Wonders Hall in '63, upper left in photo. McDonel Hall was also completed in '63 with Akers Hall and Fee Hall completed in'64, Holmes Hall in '65, and Hubbard Hall in '66.

wristwatch, threw it into the concrete mixer, jumped back into the car, and took off. Bill asked, "Who the heck was that?" Someone replied, "Oh, that was Vince Vandenburg."

When Vince arrived, our department reorganized to address the huge workload of new, large construction projects. The lower level of the Physical Plant office wing was fitted out to house the team of senior engineers and the full-time field construction inspectors. All the senior engineers moved downstairs, many new faces were hired, and Bob Siefert joined the group as the lone architect. Don Ross transferred from Campus Park and Planning (formerly the Site Planning office) and became the manager, with the remaining engineering staff left upstairs. Shortly after, though, he left MSU and returned to private practice.

Vince ended up becoming something of a counselor to me. We would frequently go to lunch together, and he would tell me many stories about his student days as a football player at MSC, stories about John Hannah, and even stories about Gen. George Patton, as Vince commanded an Engineering battalion during World War II and built bridges for the advancing Third Army.

One day, Vince was chuckling that he had two old campus lanterns up at his cottage at Good Heart, even though no one was to have one. He explained that they came off the Farm Lane Bridge when the sidewalks were widened. He further explained that the lanterns were unique to MSU and therefore were not to be sold or distributed to the general public. (I gathered that this edict was a John Hannah "rule" and that Vince enjoyed "special dispensation.")

■   ■   ■

A new power plant was under construction, requiring the installation of a steam tunnel from the plant to the campus. However, the tunnel would have to cross under railroad tracks owned by the Grand Trunk/Canadian National Railroad, and permission could only be granted by Ted Jacobs, chief engineer for the railroad. (The Grand Trunk Railroad is the two-rail main line from Montreal to Chicago, and the staff would frequently remind us that they were established by a grant from the Queen of England and thus were sovereign.) Vince and I went to Detroit and met with Jacobs, who asked how I planned to install the new tunnel. I said, "Jacking a large steel tube." (Jacking a tube under roads or railroad is a fairly common construction practice. One digs a large hole next to the road and installs large hydraulic pistons or jacks to push the lubricated tube sections, one after another, under the road. Each tube section is welded to the previous tube section as it's lowered into the jacking pit.)

Jacobs said, "No. I'll only approve the crossing if you use liner plates, which is our normal practice." Obviously, we had to agree if we were going to receive the railroad's permission.

Liner plates are curved steel plates, approximately 12 inches wide and 24 inches long, with flanges on all sides to allow connecting all adjacent plates with bolts. Bolting liner plates in connecting rings requires a beam to hold up the top of the next ring as it's being installed and bolted to the previously installed ring. The far end of the beam has to rest on a mount sitting out beyond the rings.

Holden Hall, under construction in '66 and completed in '67, was the last of the large undergraduate dormitories. Owen Graduate Hall was also completed in '61 with an addition in '65. Each of these dormitories, built during the 1960s, housed approximately 1,200 students. In total, nearly 10,000 additional beds were made available.

Unfortunately, during construction, crews hit a pocket of loose soil, causing the support beam to fall, which in turn undermined the integrity of the rails above. This required all trains to operate under "slow orders" until the crossing was completed. Jacobs, of course, couldn't have known that would happen if we followed his orders. But it nevertheless was rewarding when, during a meeting with him after the crossing was completed, Jacobs said, "Next time, Flinn, we'll do it your way."

The rapid campus expansion along with the ever-increasing number of students revealed the need for a campus bus system. It was determined that Physical Plant would take on the responsibility and have it operating by fall term 1964. We hired an experienced bus system manager who knew how we could obtain used buses in Colorado and also how to develop bus routes. This low-cost system served MSU for 35 years.

On November 18, 1964, our son James was born.

During this period, I functioned as a staff engineer, designing the utilities to connect new buildings to the existing trunk lines, as well as smaller buildings and additions such as the salvage yard building, recently removed for the new Capital Area Multimodel Gateway, and many farm structures, such as the Botany Field Lab (now known as the Plant Pathology Research Center) on College Road. Bob Siefert and I designed the Tree Research complex on Jolly Road and the Beaumont Nursery, installing campus well #20 in the corner of the head house as a bit of economy. This approach supplied the nursery with water and, at the same time, added capacity to serve our expanding campus without building a separate well house. (As we installed more and more major campus wells out into the farm district, we would abandon the small wells serving the nearby farm facility, as the big wells caused the small wells to go dry.)

There were numerous other challenges, including designing the irrigation system for the "duffers" golf course east of Harrison Road and producing such studies as a report on central water softening.

Living across the street from Don and Audrey Cross, and with our girls being the same age, we all became very close friends. It made no difference to any of us that the Flinn family happened to be white and the Cross family happened to be black.

One evening, the four of us adults decided to go to dinner at Tarpoff's, one of the best restaurants during that era. After being seated, I was shocked to hear racist comments being uttered by the occupants of some of the other tables, loud enough so Don and Audrey could hear them. The Crosses were very composed, acting just as if they had not heard the nasty rhetoric. I was exceedingly proud of their reaction and absolutely appalled by the actions of the obviously prejudiced individuals in the room. Sadly, I had to admit that racism was alive and well in Lansing.

With Power Plant '65 coming on line in late 1965, the old North Campus Power Plant could be removed. I was assigned to be the project manager, designer, and field inspector for the project. The first step was to design a large underground vault to house the electrical gear serving the North Campus buildings. After all the equipment was moved from the second floor to the new vault, the large air compressors needed to be relocated to the mechanical system basement. Then demolition began. Dropping the 185-foot

Power Plant '65 (now known as T. B. Simon Power Plant) was completed in 1965. Note the Quonset huts that were recycled as construction offices.

smoke stack was the most dramatic part of that exercise. The demolition was also symbolic: Since 1922, the smoke stack bore the letters "MAC" in white bricks, a long-standing reminder of the school's origin as Michigan Agricultural College that had dominated the campus. Very few people knew that we also had to remove an underground water reservoir. That project required the removal of the boilers, coal bunkers, railroad tracks, and railroad bridge over the river. All this major surgery took place without any extended utility outage. This project was one of my more successful, as I buried the remaining components of a power plant and left nothing showing above ground. (It is worth pointing out that access to the underground chambers is via a door flush with the ground that opens using a key box mounted on a nearby light pole. I call this access my "Bela Lugosi door," in honor of the famous actor who was the first to portray Count Dracula and starred in many other horror movies.)

The completion of Power Plant '65 allowed the removal of the obsolete North Campus Power Plant and its chimney, which had the iconic MAC (Michigan Agricultural College) white bricks. This site is now the front lawn of the John A. Hannah Administration Building.

The removal of the North Campus Power Plant also removed the irrigation pump that had pushed water to Beal Gardens and beyond. The solution was to retain the water intake facility located along the Red Cedar River, which had originally been built to supply condensing water to the electrical turbines at the power plant. I installed high-pressure pumps in the intake building and reconnected the underground piping so we could continue to use river water for irrigation. A related conversion was to reuse the potable water mains feeding the barrack housing north of Shaw Lane by reconnecting them to the irrigation system. This provided a very low-cost but adequate irrigation system. This area is now known as Munn Field.

Another interesting assignment was salvaging Pewabic Pottery. MSU acquired the Pewabic Pottery building in Detroit, once the home to a company internationally known for the unique iridescent glazes on their architectural tiles, during 1964. The building was in disrepair. I was asked to put it back into a functioning condition. I hired Fidel Cashero, of Grunwell Cashero, to remove one broken kiln, repair the wall, and replace the roof. (Fidel first worked at MSC when he had only a pickup truck and one swing stage, a scaffold-style work platform that can be lowered down the face of a building.) MSU transferred the building to the nonprofit Pewabic Society in 1981. Today, the building is a National Historic Landmark.

On July 1, 1966, I was given the opportunity to prove that I could run the upstairs Engineering office and began reporting directly to Ted Simon. The full-time staff was three draftsmen—Max Seeds, Don Cross, and Marv Montgomery—estimator Luther Whipple, and secretary Donna Irish. I could also hire as many students as I needed. Six months later, Luther Whipple died unexpectedly. After attempting to have numerous individuals pick up the estimating role along with designing, it became obvious we needed a replacement for Whip. Don Cross was the best answer. He served in that role until his retirement in 1995.

Also during 1966, my classification at MSU changed to Administrative Professional, which provided much more security than the labor payroll and allowed participation in TIAA-CREF (Teachers Insurance and Annuity Association—College Retirement Equities Fund).

In 1967, Holden Hall, the last of the new residence halls, was completed along with Wells Hall, Parking Ramp #2, Baker Hall, and a major addition to the library. The new Administration, Music Practice, and Laundry buildings were under construction as well. Even so, it was clear that the great construction boom that began in 1963 was coming to an end.

MSU had successfully replaced the old temporary facilities, and the goals for higher education on the part of the State and Federal government had, for the most part, been met. Many of the senior engineers who were reviewing new construction plans left for other challenges or returned to the design firms they had left before coming to MSU. Most of the highly experienced construction inspectors found opportunities in the private sector.

During 1967, I was able to achieve a major personal goal: I became a licensed professional engineer (PE) in Michigan. I was also given the opportunity to attend a workshop of the National Association of Physical Plant Administrators (NAPPA) held in Akron, Ohio. That experience had a profound impact upon me. I still remember two of the instructors: J. McCree Smith from North Carolina State University and James Wenner from the University of Cincinnati, both physical plant directors and past presidents of NAPPA. It led me to believe that maybe my future would best be served as a physical plant director at a major institution. With that in mind, I completed a degree in business management from LaSalle Extension University. That would be useful for me since plant directors are, essentially, business managers overseeing a collection of businesses.

■　■　■

One day, Ted Simon came to my office and said we needed to meet with his boss, Vice President Phil May. After we arrived at his office, May said, "Ron, as you know we're planning to build a faculty club on Forest Road, and we need city utilities. I also understand you live on Forest Road." (In April 1967, I had become a charter member of the proposed MSU faculty club. I couldn't lose out by having someone else build, maintain, and operate a swimming pool across the street while Norene and I were raising three small kids.)

"Well," May went on, "when the City of Lansing heard MSU was planning to buy all the land east of I-127, they dropped plans to extend water and sewer under the expressway. As a resident of the area, I think you would be the perfect one to convince the city to extend those utilities."

Of course, the only appropriate response was, "Yes, sir."

I quickly learned that utilities get extended only if a majority of the affected property owners sign a petition, or if owners of 51 percent of the front footage sign. In order to obtain signatures from a majority of the owners, we had to agree to subsidize a portion of their assessments. That led Lee Cross, Don's father, to accuse me of "buying off my neighbors." This was a bit awkward: my children referred to Lee as "Grampa Cross," and he and I had become good friends. For whatever reason, he was opposed to the project and told people that "drunken professors will be driving up and down Forest Road" as they went to and from the club. In spite of these protests, the University Club *was* built. (As it happened, his granddaughters, Regina and Felicia, along with my daughters, Beth and Lisa, ended up working together to sell lemonade to the construction workers.)

■　■　■

In late 1967, a rift between two members of the Board of Trustees and the university's administration became public. The two trustees were calling for Phil May's dismissal. Many thought their real goal was to get John Hannah to step down or retire and that they were getting at him through discrediting May, who was a key member of the president's inner circle.

There was even more turmoil brewing.

It became widely known that Vince Vandenburg was Hannah's brother-in-law. Newspaper articles alleged that that personal relationship made Vandenburg's working relationship with MSU inappropriate at the very least. He decided to leave the university to eliminate any more embarrassment to the president. Around this time, he wasn't feeling well. He went to his cottage, which usually worked as a tonic, but it did not help. Doctors finally suggested exploratory surgery, which revealed a cancer that had spread throughout his abdomen. He died soon after.

I know that many people were not pleased with Vince's "hell-bent for leather" style. To be honest, he could be careless or thoughtless about how he dealt with people, sometimes even falling into the habit of using coarse language. He just didn't always take the time to consider his words or reflect on the impression he was making; there was too little time and too much to be done. And he did get things done.

There were many inspirational quotes that he frequently repeated; two that I remember and use with some frequency are "Have you noticed how hard the lucky ones *work* at it?" and "When the going gets tough, the tough get going." He also placed a large sign in his office that read, "What's Best for MSU?" It is a phrase the MSU facilities team still uses today.

With Vince's passing, the responsibility for major field inspection was transferred to me as part of the newly renamed Engineering Services department.

Meanwhile, the trustee battle raged on. In time, it took its toll. Effective March 1, 1968, Phil May requested a leave of absence. Roger Wilkinson was named assistant vice president, with authority to act for May. On November 30, May's leave of absence turned into an official retirement. The next day, Wilkinson became acting vice president for Business and Finance. Seventeen months later, he became vice president.

Even Roger was surprised that he was picked to replace Phil since there were other candidates who were older and had more experience. I believe a major factor in Roger's selection was that he had offended very few people. In a sometimes heated and highly political university environment, that is no small thing. This event, along with other experiences and observations, has caused me to develop a philosophy: "Don't tick off any more people on a given day than necessary, as they may get the chance to vote!"

■　■　■

In May 1968, Ted Simon and I went to see Jack Breslin, who was secretary of the Board of Trustees and secretary of the university, viewed by many as holding the number-two position on campus. Jack told us that MSU had decided that the computer lab needed a new CDC 6500 computer installed before fall term. And I, of course, needed to make it happen. I told Jack that we needed a whole new HVAC system, the project would have to be fast-tracked to meet the deadline, and that I couldn't have anyone—including Purchasing or auditors—delaying the process by challenging my decisions and directives. He said, "You have it." I and my team delivered.

In June 1968, the National District Heating Association asked me to present my paper on "Walk-Through Steam Tunnels at Michigan State University" at their annual meeting in Bellaire, Michigan, of all places. This organization held its annual meetings throughout the United States. But the year I'm invited to speak, it's in Michigan. So I got to drive up to Bellaire in the morning and drive home in the afternoon instead of going to some really nice spot, like San Diego.

■　■　■

On the evening of February 11, 1969, John Hannah delivered his annual "State of the University" address in Fairchild Theatre. But it turned out to be his farewell address as well. I and a few others arrived just a few minutes before he was to speak. Because of the large attendance, we were seated on the stage behind him. His voice was so low that we could hear the distant sound of glass windows being broken by rocks thrown by the several hundred student demonstrators outside who were protesting the Vietnam War.

I felt it was a great honor to have served on the John Hannah team as we transformed this great institution. He was a university president whose shadow was far bigger than even that of Michigan's governor.

Hannah went on to become director of the federal Agency for International Development. Walter Adams was appointed acting president on April 1, 1969.

Looking back over all that took place during the 1960s—doubling the square footage of permanent buildings, including many residence halls (which made MSU the largest university housing program in the nation); relocating all the farm units south of Mount Hope Road; extending Shaw Lane to Hagadorn Road; creating Wilson Road; constructing a state-of-the-art cogenerating power plant; along with adding the expansive utility extensions and removing the old North Campus Plant—I had to admit that this had been an exciting and challenging journey for a young engineer at the start of his professional career. Little did I realize that the next decade would present me with a whole new array of challenges.

The Transformed University

A s dramatic as the physical growth was during the 1960s, MSU also ex-perienced a metamorphosis regarding campus culture and employee relations.

President John Hannah was viewed as ruling with an iron fist, even described by some as a "benevolent despot." (I was amazed to be told early on that Hannah did not acknowledge nor allow employee coffee breaks, believing them to be a waste of time.) But many of the new faculty and employees joining MSU during the '60s were from a different generation—and thought differently—than the president. There were bound to be challenges to the status quo. In a 1999 interview with *The State News,* former Provost John Cantlon recalled, "Most of the faculty applauded what Hannah had done but recognized that the university had matured and would do better with a little democracy in the system."

By 1969, all employee groups had unionized or had representation re-garding employment conditions, except for the faculty and the administrative professional (AP) staff. This abruptly changed when Acting President Walter Adams summarily fired both the Wilson Hall manager and food service manager, during what became known as the "Midnight Massacre" to settle a student protest. Up to that point, AP employees had shown no interest in unions or organizing. But at a meeting in the Kellogg Center Auditorium held two days after the "massacre," I knew that had changed; the auditorium was full, and I thought, *This dog is going to hunt.*

University Budget Officer Lowell Levi and I were convinced the APs would be best served by an association rather than a union, and we volunteered to write the bylaws. We were successful when Secretary to the Board of Trustees Jack Breslin agreed to give it a try. Subsequently, I became chair of the Salary and Benefits committee. (I am especially proud of the fact that I got Jack to agree that MSU should assist employees in gaining additional education. My former employer Union Carbide had encouraged its employees to gain additional education by providing tuition reimbursement. At that time, MSU, on the other hand, provided no such incentives, even though it was and is one of the world's largest educational institutions.) The AP association was also effective in increasing salaries, many of which were exceedingly low; MSU was truly *Spartan* when it came to pay rates. I was told that when we had to pay Andy Hunt, the first dean of human medicine, $50,000 a year in 1965, it was discovered that John Hannah was only making $35,000 a year. He worked cheap, and we worked cheap.

To enhance new-project planning, we reactivated the Building committee in May 1969, with University Architect Bob Siefert as chair reporting directly to Jack Breslin. Thus, Bob and I became the team to decide which consulting design team should get the next MSU project. This approach continued for many years.

During the construction boom of the 1960s, the need to provide guidelines to consulting architects and engineers became all too apparent. We ended up writing the MSU Construction Standards to help consultants quickly learn the features of our utility systems and what building details assured the lowest life-cycle costs. When these standards became known by other universities, they became a "best seller" across the country.

In late fall 1969, Ted Simon told me MSU was facing a budget problem. "You and your wizards need to go out across campus and figure out how to lower our energy bill by $50,000," he said. Fortunately, Don Rodgers was part of an analysis group recently transferred to Engineering Services. Don was an electrician as well as an expert on HVAC controls. I asked him what he thought we could do. He said, "The first thing I would do is put the pins back into the

The Life Sciences Building, completed in 1971, provided much-needed research space as well as new office space for the School (now College) of Nursing.

time clocks that start and stop the ventilation fans. After being directed to change the settings a few times, for evening events and whatnot, the troops get frustrated and just pull the pins out altogether, so the fans end up running 24 hours a day. Next, we need to turn off the fans supplying and exhausting the dining rooms and kitchens in the residence halls when those areas are unoccupied." We implemented those steps, and anything else we could think of, and wound up saving $100,000. I told Don, "Write up all the things we did. You never know when we may have to do it again." (This information became known as the "Quick-fix" or "Fast and Dirty" steps shared with other universities, via APPA meetings, during the energy crisis of the 1970s.)

In October 1969, the Board of Trustees appointed Clifton R. Wharton Jr., president of MSU, effective January 1, 1970. They also amended their bylaws to establish the title of Executive Vice President of the University and Secretary of the Board of Trustees, with Jack Breslin continuing in that capacity.

Our biggest construction project during 1970 was the Life Sciences building. We relied on George Fox as an assistant project inspector during the summer months to facilitate vacation time for our senior staff. George was the basketball coach at Everett High School. He loved coaching. And one day he was particularly excited to tell us all about this kid who he was sure would become a great player. We were all saying to yourselves, "Yeah, yeah, George. *Every* coach thinks he has a rising star on his hands." But it turned out that George was correct. That student was Earvin "Magic" Johnson, who went on to become a star player at MSU, was drafted by the Los Angeles Lakers, was named one of the 50 greatest players in the history of the National Basketball Association, and even won a gold medal in the Olympics. (My future son-in-law Mark Lenhard played on the Everett High School team with "Magic.")

That summer, I took a week's vacation to work on building a new house for the Flinn family on Willoughby Road in Holt, just a mile south of MSU's southern border. My work was interrupted when I was called back to campus to attend the kickoff meeting for Unit 3 for Power Plant '65. I had been appointed project manager for Unit 3 in addition to running Engineering Services. This opportunity provided me a deeper understanding of modern power plants. It was a critical time for power plants: the newly passed Clean Air Act of 1970 would have a profound impact on coal-burning power plants in the years to come.

The Willoughby Road house project resulted from my selling our Forest Road house to MSU so it could complete a proposed research park. MSU was willing to pay an over-market price, which allowed me to buy 40 acres and build a new house. I was actually looking for just five acres so we would have the space for my children to experience the responsibility of owning a horse or pony, as I had. (Over the years, I had met several folks who got into owning horses, but then, after the charm wore off, decided they didn't like all the work and expense.) There were no five-acre plots available near MSU, so I ended up buying the 40 acres making up the west half of the old Richter farm. Years earlier, the land had supplied Richter's Gardens, which had been the go-to landscape and garden store on South Cedar Street in Lansing. Being a truck garden, though, there were no trees on the property. I decided we should plant trees to appreciate the property. I obtained low-cost seedlings each spring from the county conservation office and began planting.

A few months after we moved into the new house, tragedy struck: my stepmother, who had moved to the area, had decided to spend the night with us as she was experiencing severe heartburn. Early the next morning, she unexpectedly died. It was determined to be cardiac arrest at the age of 66.

Several years earlier, she had decided to leave Buffalo, New York, as the relationship with my father had deteriorated to the point that it caused her extreme emotional distress. Years earlier, she had told me that my dad probably married her on the rebound after losing my real mother. Some months later, she sensed that he was seeing someone else. This awkward situation existed for as long as I can remember, and when I moved to Buffalo, he was not actually living with us. My stepmother and I ended up becoming very close. When a doctor advised her to leave Buffalo for her emotional health, I offered to move her here as she had no other family.

My stepmother was Elizabeth Dixon Flinn, but she was known as Bessie. She emigrated from Scotland when she was 20 years old. She had been trained as a domestic, which made her in high demand by households who could afford such help. Fortunately, Lansing had a large number of emigrants from Scotland in the St. Andrew's Society, and she quickly developed new friends here. After a few months, she was retained by the Thomas Smith family, who lived at "Barefoot Acres" out on Williams Road and asked her to live in.

Mr. Smith was the son of George T. Smith, who had become wealthy by developing several Market Basket stores during the 1940s and 1950s. The two large Smith houses, George T.'s and Thomas's, sat next to but quite a distance apart from each other on the east side of the Grand River, separated by a large swimming pool. Mrs. Thomas Smith was the granddaughter of automotive pioneer R. E. Olds. The entire Smith family essentially adopted Bessie, and we were privileged to be frequent guests in their home, where we got to know George T. and several times met the two daughters of R. E. Olds—Mrs. Bernice Olds Roe and Mrs. Gladys Olds Anderson. Mrs. Smith was very attached to Bessie, and she even attended the second funeral for Bessie that was held in Morrisville, New York, staying with my brother Bob and his wife Shirley. (We had held a funeral here in Lansing for us and her friends in this area, but she always wanted to be buried back in Eaton, New York, and we honored her wishes.) It's ironic to have developed such a close relationship with the descendants of the individual whose name is on the first building I entered at MSU and where I had most of my engineering classes. And it probably would never have happened if Bessie had not come to live in Lansing.

In April 1971, I was asked to present my paper "Walk-Through Steam Tunnels at Michigan State University" at the fifty-eighth annual meeting of the Association of Physical Plant Administrators (APPA) held in Tucson, Arizona. This was the first time Norene or I was west of Michigan, and it was very exciting for both of us. I got to meet many of the "big names" in APPA (e.g., M. F. Fifield at the University of New Mexico) and to travel to Nogales, Mexico, for one of the dinners.

At that time, APPA had no central office or staff. Everything was done by volunteers on various campuses. Even the newsletter, which for years had been produced by Richard Adams at the University of Oregon, was done as a labor of love. (This arrangement encouraged a strong spirit of cooperation among APPA members. For example, at MSU we put together the first Physical Plant Unit Cost Comparison document for all the campuses who were willing to share their data. This was well received by university physical plants across the country.) In 1970, Gerry Hawk at Eastern New Mexico University had volunteered to serve part time as an administrative director to see if there was a need for a central office. There was. At our meeting in '71, the Professional Affairs committee recommended that an office, with a full-time administrative director, be established as a national headquarters in Washington, DC.

That was a significant moment for APPA. Another, sadder, one was around the corner.

Robert Houston, director at the University of Arizona, was president-elect for APPA and the meeting host in 1971. (It was traditional in those years for the president-elect to also host.) He mentioned how excited he was about a hunting trip into the mountains he was taking with some friends soon after the meeting. Regrettably, he became seriously ill during the trip. By the time his friends could get him out of the mountains and to a hospital, he had died. APPA officers called an emergency session and voted to appoint Ted Simon the new president-elect.

In early 1972, Ted Simon co-chaired the selection committee that chose Paul Knapp, editor of *Buildings* magazine, as the first executive director of APPA. Later that year, Ted became APPA president. Michigan State has had an intense involvement with APPA for decades. In 1939, Michigan State College hosted the annual meeting of what was then known as the Association of Superintendents of Buildings and Grounds of Universities and Colleges.

Ward A. Davenport was the host. He became president of the association the following year.

The experience of attending and presenting at the '71 APPA annual meeting further raised my interest in becoming a physical plant director at a university and becoming more active in APPA.

■ ■ ■

In May 1971, Jack Breslin informed me that MSU had decided to bring a College of Osteopathic Medicine to our campus. It would open in September, and Fee Hall needed to be renovated for the new college before the students arrived. Fee Hall was one of the modern residence halls built in the 1960s. It had a very large central kitchen, with refrigerators large enough to accommodate food carts. The kitchen needed extensive renovations to transform it into a gross-anatomy laboratory, but we discovered that a cadaver cart is very much like a food cart, which made the cooler conversion easy. Again, being given full authority, we pulled it off.

John Lewis who was head of the division's Business Procedures office was promoted and became the director of University Services. Then Ted Simon decided to transfer the Business Procedures office responsibility to me. This allowed me to become much more knowledgeable of the budgets and finances for the entire division.

The depth of engineering talent in Engineering Services was not deep, as there were only two other actual engineers on board, Shorty Noonon and Jim Easley—and Shorty was talking about retiring within a year or so. Thus, I began recruiting students who appeared to have the "right stuff" and who might be interested in staying on after graduation. Terry Ruprecht, Bob Nestle, Bob Ellerhorst, Dave Sonnega, and Van Frazee were among those individuals added to the team.

During the early 1970s, several buildings were in design or construction. The Nisbet building joined the Manly Miles building, east of Harrison Road, as a rental facility for organizations with a relationship with MSU, allowing the Personnel office to move from the Weather Bureau building (now Wills House) on Michigan Avenue. The new Public Safety building finally made it possible for the campus police to move out of the Quonset huts. It also provided MSU the ability to retain individuals in holding cells.

I also became involved with a project to build four lakes south of Jolly

Road, straddling College Road. The concept was to prove that effluent from a sewage plant, after the solids have been removed, could be purified by natural means: The aquatic plants in lakes two and three would consume the nutrients that normally cause algae blooms when released from a sewage plant directly into a river. After flowing through the first three lakes, the water in the fourth lake was expected to be of recreational quality. The primary promoters were two professors, Howard Tanner and Bob Ball. We had many meetings with various state agencies to obtain the necessary approvals. The federal grant funding the project could only be received by a city or municipality, so officially it was an East Lansing project. The lakes were fed waste water from the East Lansing sewage plant via a 20-inch diameter pipeline and the entire project was completed in 1973. (It was a privilege to get to know Howard Tanner as he was credited with introducing salmon to the Great Lakes.)

When construction bids were taken for Munn Ice Arena, they came in over budget. During the discussions of what to do, Bill Beardsley, athletic ticket manager, said he wasn't sure he could sell enough tickets to fill all the seats. Amo Bessone, hockey coach, said, "If you build a good arena, you'll be able to attract a good coach and you will not be able to build it big enough!" Ron Mason proved Amo was correct. As Ron became the most successful coach in NCAA ice hockey history, I heard many times that the biggest argument during local divorce proceedings was over who gets the hockey tickets!

The 300,000-pounds-per-hour steam boiler being designed as part of Unit 3 at Power Plant '65 required significant fly-ash emission control to satisfy the Clean Air Act. Baghouses—fabric filters for trapping pollutants released during power-plant combustion—had not yet been perfected, so a hot-gas precipitator was specified. Our design consultant, Commonwealth Associates, also recommended that Unit 3 be built to burn natural gas and #6 fuel oil as well as coal. Installing the capability to burn #6 fuel oil would have required building two 1,000,000-gallon storage tanks and a huge unloading station for tanker trucks delivering the oil. After careful consideration, we decided to delete the fuel-oil option. We have never regretted that decision. During this period, natural gas prices dropped for just a few months, allowing us to add natural-gas firing to Units 1 and 2 and pay for it with one season's fuel cost savings.

■　■　■

Munn Ice Arena, completed in 1974, finally provided a decent facility for Intercollegiate Hockey.

The federal government was interested in the expansion of medical research facilities that would also expand medical education. Our response was a new Clinical Center, which consisted of three large buildings: an office building, a clinical building, and a building housing research animals. We included a central control panel for energy-consuming systems in the construction specifications for the project.

The central control panel allows an operator at the panel to start/stop all HVAC equipment throughout the complex and assures that equipment shuts down when not needed, thereby conserving energy. The operator also can adjust the discharge temperature of the air handlers and the water temperature flowing to the various rooms. Sensors in the heating and cooling equipment are also capable of sending an alarm to the panel if a malfunction occurs. Once construction contracts were awarded, I was successful in obtaining approval from the funding federal agency to move the panel to our building since such a panel is capable of handling 30 buildings as easily as three. Our timing was fortuitous: The energy crisis was upon us; any and all conservation measures would be required. More about that in the next chapter.

Energy was not the only crisis, however. On April 20, 1975, the Red Cedar River crested at 11.75 feet, nearly six feet above flood stage. This was the night Tony Bennett and Lena Horne were scheduled to perform in the MSU Auditorium. Unfortunately, river water found its way into the auditorium basement as well as some electrical circuits, so the show was quickly moved to the Munn Ice Arena, with very little delay in starting the performance. In addition, Jenison Fieldhouse was completely surrounded by water and received extensive damage as the basement became completely flooded. Circle IM also suffered damage, but not to the same extent. This flood crest is considered a "100-year flood" and remains the highest water on record for the Red Cedar River since 1904.

During 1975, the Management Education Center for the College of Business was under construction in Troy, Michigan. Several corporations in southeastern Michigan, including General Motors, were interested in additional capacity for Executive Management of Business Administration (EMBA) training in that region. General Motors had their construction arm, Argonaut Realty, design the building. Bob Siefert dropped off a set of plans and specs and said, "It's a done deal. The president is not interested in our presenting any comments on this project." Given that we were to have no involvement, I was annoyed when Siefert called several months later and said we needed to go to Troy because there were construction issues.

"I'm not going," I said. "We were told to butt out."

"Oh, you're going," Bob said.

As I suspected, within the hour Ted Simon came to my office, said Jack Breslin had just called him, and told me firmly, "You're going."

We went.

The rumor was that an underground river was eroding the soil beneath the concrete flooring, causing it to settle. But in reviewing the situation, I noticed that dirt piled on a slope next to the building site had become "liquid mud" due to a recent rainstorm and had flowed down the slope and across the concrete floor. Only portions of the floor had broken and settled, and I knew those areas were where large-diameter metal HVAC ducts had been placed below the floor. So I asked the contractors, "How did you compact the soil when you backfilled around the ducts?" There was lots of embarrassment on the part of the contractors. It turned out that the soil on site was a heavy clay, which when dry resembled pebbles and appeared to adequately perform as backfill. Once it was saturated by the "liquid mud" seeping through cracks in the concrete floor, though, it shrank significantly, causing the floor slab to break and fall. Properly compacted sand would have been a better choice. (I couldn't help but remember the Wilson Road incident I'd gone through just a few years earlier. Why don't more contractors appreciate the importance of properly compacting backfill? Why don't more engineers recognize the need for rigorous specifications?) In this case, the contractor had to remove the floor, remove the poor fill, replace it with properly compacted backfill, and replace the floor. Given this issue and other design concerns, I was pleased that I was not directly responsible for delivering this project.

After months of trying, I finally succeeded in obtaining permission to add a licensed architect to the Engineering Services staff. Jack Breslin wanted assurance that we wouldn't infringe on the authority of Bob Siefert, university architect. I was able to show that we had many small projects that needed the talents of an architect, and Bob didn't have time to help. So I hired Don Freed. With his help, we completed the stair tower addition on the north side of the Human Ecology building, added handicapper access to the museum, expanded the fire station on Shaw Lane, and removed the front steps of Cowles House.

As the end of the decade approached, we began one last major project. Our president's wife, Mrs. Dolores Wharton, took a great interest in MSU building a decent performance hall to replace the auditorium, which was wanting in terms of both sight lines and acoustics. During one conceptual meeting with the architectural firm, she stated, "I realize we may not be able to afford a Cadillac. But we must at least have a Buick!" It would be several years before we would put the finishing touches on the Wharton Center for the Performing Arts, but I believe Mrs. Wharton's vision and our efforts paid off in a grand way. I would suggest that the building that bears the Wharton name *is* a Cadillac.

Energy, Accessibility, and Enhancements

A s you may have gathered from the previous chapter, the 1970s were not years of dramatic expansion in terms of either building projects or overall vision for MSU's future. My department was focused mainly on reactive solutions to the decade's challenges, while providing basic maintenance and modest enhancements to aging structures. But there are several significant areas in which MSU was proactive—to the point where we became an example to institutions across the country.

Today, it's difficult to remember just how big a deal the 1970s energy crisis was. President Jimmy Carter was on national television telling all of us what we needed to do to help in this national crisis—from reducing automobile usage to adjusting our home thermostats. Congress directed the American Council on Education (ACE) to get universities to do their part in energy reduction. ACE turned to the National Association of College and University Business Officers (NACUBO) and APPA. Michigan State University already had a reputation as a prudent energy consumer, which led to Ted Simon being named to a national, seven-member energy task force. Power Plant '65 became a mecca for various institutions and companies across the nation. This highly efficient cogenerating facility, firing an abundant native fuel, was the envy of many; there was a very real fear that both natural gas and fuel oil would be rationed. The federal government even passed a law that prohibited any coal-fired power plant being converted to natural gas. At this critical time, coal was once again "king."

On campus, President Wharton issued numerous requests and directives for reducing energy consumption over several years. Reductions did occur, although many people on campus were unhappy with cooler room temperatures in winter and higher temperatures in summer. Yet, in 1974 alone, these steps yielded a savings of $500,000.

With the installation of the central control panel in the Physical Plant building, we were afforded a heightened measure of control over electrical usage throughout a large section of campus. Once it was installed, we started connecting other campus buildings to the network. Housing and Food Services were keenly interested in reducing their utility bills and were financially able to fund the first cable extensions to their buildings. (It is worth noting that we ran three cables, even though only one was needed for energy control; interest in cable TV and the Internet, which began as a way of networking universities long before it became popular for the general public, was on the horizon.) Being able to shut off unneeded HVAC systems from a central panel—along with a cogeneration power plant capable of burning whichever fuel is cheaper—has provided MSU an annual cost avoidance of many millions of dollars.

I think it is interesting that MSU at this time was more attuned to energy-reduction measures than some of those who supposedly were overseeing MSU's efforts. During design of the Clinical Center, for example, we recommended that lighting levels in classrooms be 50 foot-candles, the MSU standard. The funding agency said their standard was 100 foot-candles. If we didn't add the additional lighting, they would consider canceling the project altogether. We of course capitulated. But after the project was completed, we went in and removed half of the fluorescent tubes! Later, in addressing the energy crisis, federal standards were reduced to 50 foot-candles.

As the Unit 3 power plant neared completion, clean-air regulations required emission reductions on Units 1 and 2. Lengthy, drawn-out discussions within the state legislature led the regulatory agencies to remind MSU that continued pollution at earlier levels was in violation of federal law and could lead to serious consequences. Finally, the State of Michigan elected to add this work to the Unit 3 project as it had agreed to fund the emission controls on Units 1 and 2 as well as Unit 3. By this time, baghouses had been proven effective for reducing pollution, following the development of Teflon-coated fiberglass bags that could withstand the high flue-gas temperatures. The Unit 3 project ended up taking a decade to complete, with the final payment issued in 1980.

■　■　■

MSU's commitment to providing equal access to a university education for all students led to the establishment of the Office of Programs for Handicapped Students in 1971–72, with Judy Gentile as director. (MSU was proactive in this regard, as the Americans with Disabilities Act did not become law until 1990.) Judy's husband Eric, who was himself in a wheelchair, also was an effective spokesperson for accessibility and attended our planning meetings. Eric was a staff member of the Office of Programs for Handicapped Students and was able to read blueprints. He significantly participated in the design process for new and renovation projects.

Judy and Eric convinced the university to install curb cuts and modify housing units and classroom buildings to achieve accessibility for wheelchair users, but it seemed that we could always do more. Eric and I had many discussions where he pointed out how much of the campus still needed to be modified. One day, he mentioned that clearing snow from handicapper parking spaces should be a priority, and that heated sidewalks and parking spaces should also become the norm.

When I heard that, I joked, "You know, it might be less costly for handicappers to receive scholarships to Arizona State and get out of the Snow Belt!"

It wasn't a joking matter for Eric. He looked at me seriously and said, "You know, Flinn, that kind of thinking was what started the cattle cars rolling toward Auschwitz."

I decided I wasn't going to win that argument.

Also on Eric's Want List was a handicapped-accessible campus bus fleet. I was unaware of any such buses being available, but he said the University of Illinois had them.

Soon after that conversation, I attended an APPA workshop in New Orleans on "Developing an Accessible Campus for the Handicapped." There I met the chap from Illinois who developed the U of I bus fleet. He told me that the handicapper features on their buses were all hand built and had significant maintenance issues.

During our discussion, he realized I was from MSU and exclaimed, "Other than my buses, your campus is way ahead of any other campus in the country when it comes to accessibility." I then realized Judy and Eric were extremely effective advocates for their cause. When accessible vans became commercially available, we began adding them to our fleet.

■　■　■

At this time, Michigan State's cost for long-distance telephone service was rising rapidly. Attempts to significantly lower it were thwarted by the antiquated Michigan Bell switch serving MSU and the City of East Lansing. I knew about a Least Cost Routing (LCR) device that would solve our problem but required the installation of a Centrex II switch. Michigan Bell was always jumping behind the "tariff bush" whenever we asked them to replace the old switch with Centrex II. This was back in the era when "Ma Bell" had a monopoly on all telephone service; whenever a customer asked for a concession, the quick response was, "The tariff language will not allow that!" Ted and I met with Russ Krausfeldt of Comsul Ltd. in Chicago, who had spent years working for Illinois Bell, was extremely knowledgeable about tariff rules, and knew what we could and could not do. He was able to develop a specification for an MSU-owned Centrex II. When I laid that specification in front of Herb Shaw, the Michigan Bell representative, and told him we were going to issue it for bidding, he asked, "Can you give me two weeks?" I agreed. Within a week, he returned and said, "Michigan Bell will install a Centrex II to serve MSU and East Lansing." After installation of Centrex II and the LCR device, MSU's long-distance phone bill dropped by $450,000 annually.

■　■　■

In 1977, MSU President Clifton Wharton resigned to become chancellor of the State University of New York (SUNY) system. Ed Harden was named acting president on October 23, 1977. He was formally named president on March 31, 1978, but he made it clear he would stay in that position only until a successor could be found.

There were some distinct benefits to having a temporary president.

In the early 1960s, it was clear that Cowles House would benefit from

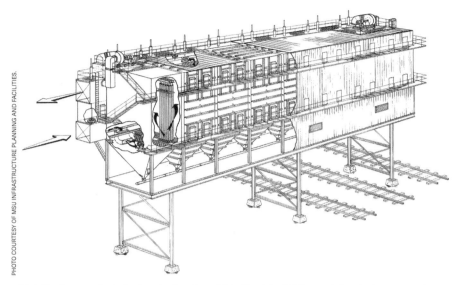

The Baghouses installed on boilers 1 and 2 in the late 1960s contained a huge number of bags, hung upside down, allowing the fly ash to be captured as the flue gases flowed up through the chambers. Once the bags reached capacity, a reverse air system would cause the bags to dump the fly ash into the hoppers below.

central air conditioning. Although Cowles House is the president's residence, its main use is as a reception center for many large events held each year. I knew the guests involved would welcome air conditioning. But I also knew the house would require a system far larger than what is required for most private homes. So I met with then President Hannah to explain what would be involved in installing central air. Upon hearing the cost estimate, though, he said firmly, "We're not doing it." Hannah suspected that the local media would write it up as "Hannah feathers his own nest!"

President Harden had no such concerns. When the upgrade was proposed to him in 1978, he said, "Let's do it. The media can't hurt me!"

■   ■   ■

On a Friday afternoon during September 1978, less than two weeks before the students were to return for fall term, a fire broke out atop the cooling tower serving power plant Units 1 and 2. (Without cooling water, the turbine generators can only produce a very small amount of electricity). In a hastily called meeting with our risk manager and our insurance company, I pointed out how much it would cost to buy power from the local power company if we were unable to produce our own. The insurance company representative said, "Do whatever it takes to get the tower rebuilt as soon as possible."

With this "blank-check authorization," I thought we stood a chance of succeeding.

Joe Kavanagh called the tower manufacturer. They said, "The guy you need just pulled into Chicago. We'll tell him to start driving to your campus immediately."

He arrived by midnight, and we met at the power plant. He first asked, "How did you prevent the fans, gear boxes, and motors from falling down through the fill?" (The "fill" is the wooden latticework through which the water cascades, becoming cooled as large volumes of air are drawn up through it.) I explained that Hi-Ball Crane Company had quickly dispatched a crane and that members of our Physical Plant skilled trades had performed some heroics that would have shocked the inspectors at OSHA.

"You just saved three weeks in time to rebuild this tower," he said.

He picked up the telephone and woke up a chap in Kentucky, who was very knowledgeable about our particular cooling tower. The man said, "I'll start assembling all the lumber needed to replace all the material above the water line. The truck will leave as soon as we can load it." The next morning, we were able to reach the fan manufacturer and placed an emergency order for six fans, including shrouds, gear boxes, and motors. They would be placed on a semi-trailer with two drivers who would drive nonstop from Oklahoma to campus. I negotiated a cost-plus contract with Chas. Featherly Construction Company, who immediately went to work removing debris and preparing the upper tower area for reconstruction. The truck and trailer with the lumber from Kentucky arrived Monday morning, and the contractor started rebuilding. The semi arrived from Oklahoma on Wednesday and reinstallation of the fans began.

On the following Friday we had the tower rebuilt and five fans running. Our risk manager arrived and said, "Ron, last Friday you said you thought it was possible to have the tower rebuilt before the students arrived. Well, you should know that everyone else was sure it couldn't happen."

■   ■   ■

It is the responsibility of the Physical Plant to keep our buildings safe, but from time to time we need to directly address student safety as well. When concerns for student safety arise—particularly with regard to walking on campus at night—we take steps to address the issue.

During the 1970s, pressure was building to install emergency phones across the campus. Specifically, we were encouraged to copy the installation in place at Wayne State University, which was called the "blue-light system" as the phone box was hung on a light fixture with a blue bulb glowing at night to reveal its location. Ted Simon told me he had seen a similar installation at the University of Washington, with the panel containing an emergency push button mounted in an attractive brass box. He asked that I find the source for the boxes. When I contacted the University of Washington, their representative laughed and said, "Those boxes were the call boxes between the bridge and boiler room on some World War II–era war ships that were scrapped a few year ago. We took all the boxes available!" We, therefore, had to locate and purchase similar equipment, which resulted in our installing a *green*-light system by December 1979.

■   ■   ■

Employee compensation had been an ongoing issue for MSU and its employees. It was a major topic in the early union bargaining sessions during the 1960s as well as during the "meeting and conferring" sessions with the AP association.

During 1972–73, MSU retained the firm of Robert H. Hayes & Associates from Chicago to develop a uniform salary program for professional and administrative employees. This effort provided some relief for employees with college degrees, but it gave little credit for long years of experience and deep institutional knowledge. In the Engineering office, this meant that there were three employees whose salaries were overtly low: Max Neils, a senior project inspector with three years of education toward a BS in Agricultural Engineering; Don Cross, an experienced architectural designer and chief estimator; and Don Rogers, an electrician who had developed deep knowledge in HVAC systems and controls. I argued that each of these individuals was more valuable than a graduate engineer with three years' experience, and I proposed a new classification, Planner-Inspector-Analyst, with an appropriate salary.

The staff person in charge of classifications at the Central Personnel office was adamantly opposed to the change.

Finally, in late 1979, I decided to talk with Gerry O'Connor, an old friend and assistant director of personnel, who was unaware of the proposal or the posture of his staff person. After listening to my story and learning which employees I was talking about, Gerry said, "I know those folks, and I think you're right." This is another example of the power of relationships; soon after, my proposed classification was put in place. It is my understanding that many other physical plants across the United States have since adopted this classification at their institutions.

■　　■　　■

Not all of the changes on campus were as visible as new construction. I noticed changes occurring behind the scenes that threatened to hamper if not derail much of the work we were trying to do. They took a toll on productivity and morale, and they led me to question whether MSU was still where I wanted to invest my time and energy.

The unionization of certain employee groups during the '60s at times created animosity and hard feelings. That negative atmosphere would linger for many years. It was easy to forget the need for a team approach when the troops wanted to emulate the then combative United Auto Workers (UAW) union and, with some regularity, called for strikes or work stoppages.

My experience with an engineer I'll just call "Howie" was only one example of what was happening on campus. Howie came on board in 1963 with experience representing management in negotiations between electrical contractors and the International Brotherhood of Electrical Workers. By 1966, virtually all units of the division, other than Engineering and Construction Inspection, reported to Howie. Many people were convinced he would be picked to replace Ted Simon if Ted left. As time went by, I realized that would be a serious mistake: Howie made a concerted effort to discourage members of his team from working with or even contacting folks in Engineering for advice or help. This went on for many years, with Howie encouraging an "us versus them" attitude among staff that was exactly the opposite of the teamwork that had previously existed.

Achieving wheelchair accessibility in buildings with split foyers (upon passing through the entrance door, one must go down or up a set of stairs) is always challenging and many times requires a large ramp. The MSU facilities team employed an ingenious approach by converting the third window, to the right of the front entrance of the Museum, with a motorized door that allows entrance to the lower level with no steps. The architecture of the building has been maintained to the point that the alteration must be pointed out to most visitors.

To be honest, the school was changing from the institution I had known ever since I had arrived in 1957. I was wrestling with whether it was time for me to adapt and stay or move on to perhaps bigger and better opportunities elsewhere.

In 1975, Bill Rouge, a fellow engineer who held a key position in the House Fiscal Agency of the State of Michigan, told me he had recommended me for the vacant physical plant director position at Eastern Michigan University. This was a great compliment. It pleased my ego to think I might possibly become a director this early in my career. I believed I was the leading candidate. During the interview, I suggested that the salary being offered was a bit low. I thought I was being subtle, but I may have chilled the vice president interviewing me. Soon after, I was notified that Bob Romkena got the job.

A year later, Charlie Birget, a senior consulting engineer and close friend, sent me a copy of a letter congratulating Romkena on moving up from physical plant director to become vice president, replacing the fellow who had interviewed me. Charlie added a personal note to my copy of the letter: "See what you missed?" It never feels good to lose, but missing out on the opportunity to become a university vice president was certainly a bit depressing. Of course, who can say whether my own work trajectory would have been the same as Romkena's even if I had been hired by EMU?

Some months later, as my family was visiting relatives while vacationing in central New York, I mentioned this experience to my brother-in-law, Wayne Smith, who is a sports nut and a great fan of MSU athletics. When I finished, Wayne turned to me and said, "Where the hell is Eastern Michigan University?!" After a lot of thought, I had to agree: To many people, being university engineer at Michigan State University is more prestigious than being vice president at a lesser-known institution.

Still, the opportunities continued to arise. In early 1978, Ted Simon pulled me aside and asked, "Are you going to apply for that physical plant job at Notre Dame?"

"Ted," I said, "that's a Catholic university. I'm a Methodist."

He just shrugged. "Oh, they're very ecumenical down there."

I therefore applied and, after two interviews, I became one of two finalists. I was told it took two extra weeks to make the decision, but Don Diedrick won. He was older and already a plant director at a small campus in DC. (Being passed over by Eastern Michigan was one thing. *This* was really depressing, as Notre Dame is as prestigious as they come. Even my brother-in-law would agree!)

Shortly after, two on-campus positions were posted and, with Ted Simon's encouragement, I applied. The first one was director of Land Management, responsible for the farm district and all the property and facilities away from East Lansing out across the state. The second position was director of Campus Park and Planning, as Milt Baron was retiring.

In both cases I was informed from a high level that MSU was best served by my remaining university engineer and that I had a good future here.

However, I knew there was no guarantee I would be picked to replace Ted Simon. Besides, there was no indication Ted was even planning to leave or retire in the near future.

I was not willing to let others' decisions determine the course for my own career. Thus, in 1980, the open position for director of Operations and Maintenance at the University of Illinois was very attractive to me—more so when I learned the position reported to Don Wendel, vice chancellor for Administrative Affairs, whom I first met when he was director of Plant Operations at the University of Michigan. I vigorously pursued this opportunity, and was successful.

However, it turned out I was offered this position just as my son was picked as starting quarterback for his high school football team. When I brought my "good news" home, Norene said, "You're really not going to do that to your son, are you?"

I had a three-day weekend to agonize. This kind of big-time position doesn't open up all that often. On the other hand, I knew that being starting quarterback was a *huge* assignment for a high school student.

I turned down the U of I offer. My decision was based on my clearly remembering who the starting quarterback was when I was in high school. (All the guys envied the starting quarterback, as all the gals swooned over him.) I don't know who the school principal was, but I remember the quarterback. I wanted to give my son that level of prestige.

The positive outcome of the U of I experience was that it became well known that I was qualified to become a plant director at a major institution.

The negative outcome: I had to put up with Howie and his influence for a few more months. Throughout the 1970s, his continuing "siloing" efforts and adversarial approach caused divisiveness between various units of the division and especially Building Services, Maintenance (trade shops), and Custodial, personified by members of Maintenance referring to the custodians as "cuspidors." The morale in the custodial ranks continued to deteriorate to where productivity in some buildings was nearly nonexistent. In November 1979, Howie requested reassignment to senior engineer, in charge of field construction inspection. He held that position for a year or so before moving on.

Of course, change is a fact of life for any university. And while Howie's departure was to be a minor improvement in the overall life of the campus, a bigger change had occurred only a few months earlier when Cecil Mackey was named president of MSU on August 3, 1979. As it turned out, Mackey's appointment came just in time for him to confront the financial exigency that was about to fall upon Michigan and all of its institutions.

Financial Crisis

I n March 1980, the House Fiscal Agency and the Senate Fiscal Agency of Michigan issued a letter to all state-supported colleges and universities stating, "the State of Michigan is facing a very bleak [Fiscal Year] 1980–81." Further, it stated, "a reduction of this magnitude would certainly have both immediate and long-term ramifications."

Initially, the impact upon MSU was an estimated $3 million cut in state appropriations, but the state's fiscal condition kept deteriorating. At the December 1980 Board of Trustees meeting, the reduction was estimated in excess of $9 million. At that point, the trustees approved a resolution calling for an immediate five-percent cash reduction and the closing of the university for two-and-a-half days in late December, which was essentially a two-and-a-half-day layoff.

The *MSU News-Bulletin* reported the action taken by the trustees and included the impact upon the services provided by the Physical Plant division: "Office cleaning will suffer with dusting and cleaning of furniture discontinued, offices cleaned and wastebaskets emptied only once per week. . . . Two senior management positions . . . will be eliminated in Physical Plant; painting of all office interiors will be discontinued; preventive maintenance throughout the university will be reduced or discontinued."

President Cecil Mackey issued the following letter to the campus community on January 7, 1981:

A LETTER TO FACULTY, STAFF, AND STUDENTS:

The State of Michigan, its people, its economy, and its institutions are suffering severe financial stress. Governor Milliken has said that the current budget-making process may be the most difficult undertaken by Michigan in this century. Because of the reduced appropriation from the State, Michigan State University must curtail programmatic and personnel commitments. Significant financial assistance from sources outside the University is not in prospect. We are already well into the fiscal year and the problems become more significant each day.

It is imperative that decisions be made in the coming weeks as to which programs and activities of Michigan State University will be continued and which curtailed or discontinued.

A four-part budget adjustment plan for 1980–81 was approved by the Board of Trustees on December 5, 1980. This plan will resolve the cash management problem for the remainder of fiscal 1980–81 assuming no further reduction in the State appropriation for 1980–81.

Now, we must turn our best efforts to the task of planning for 1981–82. The 1980–81 budget that was approved by the Board of Trustees in September 1980 must be reduced effective July 1, 1981. The precise amount of this reduction cannot be known at this date, but the reduction may be as large as $27.0 million, could be as low as $10.0 million, and will probably be in the range of $17.0 million to $20.0 million. This type of budget adjustment requires major curtailment and elimination of programs. . . .

The future of this premier land-grant and AAU institution is at stake. The basic commitment of Michigan State University has been to excellence; that commitment must be preserved. Your thoughtful assessment and creative ideas about program curtailment and elimination and the strengthening of the quality of the University can help. There are formal avenues already open for your participation in this effort. Beyond this, you are invited to send your written suggestions by January 21, 1981. . . . The Board of Trustees passed the following resolution on February 6, 1981: "As the 1980s begin, the State of Michigan and its institutions of higher education in general, including Michigan State University, face severe fiscal problems. . . .

The Board has considered the information submitted by the President concerning the nature of the fiscal crisis. In summary, Michigan State University is severely underfunded, there is a revenue shortfall of approximately $10 million for 1980–81 and a potential budget deficit of $29.2 million for 1981–82. In view of predictions of the State economy, it is also anticipated that appropriations in future years will not be adequate to fund the University at its current program level. . . .

As expressed in our budget statement of December 5, 1980, if the University attempts to sustain all of its current programs and activities, the result would be a nonselective diminution of overall program quality. Within the context of immediate and long-term financial resources, assurance of maintaining Michigan State University's commitment to high academic quality is possible only by selected continuation and adequate funding of programs and activities essential to the central role and mission of the University."

In response, the administration reviewed in detail all expenditures of the university. They considered closing certain academic units and did close certain buildings, such as the observatory. Two swimming pools also were shut down.

A faculty committee reviewed the nonacademic side of the institution and concluded that the large Physical Plant budget likely contained plenty of "fat." They soon discovered that slightly more than half the budget was for power-plant fuel and the purchase of electricity and fuel for the farm district. After reviewing the detailed expenditures for each of the various remaining Physical Plant budgets, they concluded that no financial reductions could occur without also reducing services. We were asked to identify what services could be reduced or eliminated without the university experiencing increased costs in the future. Window washing and interior painting were two. A great number of other services experienced reduced frequencies and slower response times.

Physical Plant received a 15-percent budget reduction ($1.14 million) for 1981–82. During those two fiscal years, our full-time staff dropped by 110 employees (554 to 444), mostly in Custodial. I was very pleased we were able to accomplish this reduction through attrition, thereby avoiding forced layoffs.

* * *

In June 1981, Ted Simon asked me to assume the role of acting director of Building Services, Maintenance (Skilled Trades), and Custodial.

To become reacquainted with the custodial team, I decided to visit each building during the custodians' shifts, accompanied by their supervisor and the manager of Custodial Services, Larry Mueller.

When we appeared on the scene unannounced, the initial reaction from the custodians was, "We must be in big trouble for all this 'brass' to show up!" Once employees realized the purpose for our visit, they quickly grew comfortable and shared concerns and thoughts about how we could better serve building occupants despite the budget cuts. (This was a new experience for Larry and the supervisors, as they were never given any leadership training and only learned "boss-ism" as they moved up into supervisory roles.) With great regularity, the custodians would say, "No one at your level has ever met with us like this before." They appreciated the effort.

The tradesmen in Maintenance posed a different challenge. The senior members who knew me from the early years greeted me warmly, but the folks who came on board during and after unionization appeared to be distant and, in some cases, would not even respond to a greeting from me. It was obvious the "siloing" that had taken place over many years—with even closely tied departments refusing to cooperate or communicate—created a very unfortunate climate. (I knew that the Maintenance and Custodial teams had become disenfranchised, but I was shocked to learn the plumbers didn't know the electricians, even though they punched in side by side every day.)

I obviously had a major challenge if I was going to develop a team environment and enhance service delivery to the campus.

■　■　■

Ted Simon, as mentioned earlier, was deeply involved with APPA and encouraged my involvement in the Michigan Society of Professional Engineers (MSPE). He felt the more different organizations we belonged to the better. I joined when I became licensed in 1967 and served on committees focused on student scholarships.

In 1980, John O'Malia, a fellow PE, vigorously urged me to serve as vice president of the local MSPE chapter, Grand Valley (now known as Capital Area), which led to my becoming chapter president during 1981–82. We had

The Duffy Daugherty Building has received many alterations and additions since its completion in 1980, including the indoor football practice field '85, Athletics Hall of Fame and new locker rooms '97, Clara Bell Smith Student-Athlete Academic Center '98, and the Skandalaris Addition in 2008.

a very active year that included a bus tour to the Zilwaukee Bridge project, an Engineers Convocation at which we hosted US Senator Donald Riegle, various meetings with state and local politicians, and several energetic and successful committees.

Each chapter president is responsible for developing an annual report that is evaluated at the annual MSPE meeting. We had taken pictures of most of our outings, and I thought it would be great to include them in my annual report. However, the chapter did not have the budget for a glossy publication.

One Saturday morning, as I sat in my office looking at the various committee reports and a shoebox full of pictures, I decided to see if the new copy machine (which was on trial loan to us, as it was quite expensive) could reproduce a black-and-white photo with sufficiently high quality. Our previous copy machine could not. Surprisingly, the loaner machine did it! Using my experience from the *Courier-Express,* I was able to insert pictures, with brief captions below, and assemble a nice booklet. I then made sure it bore a green-and-white cover (a little poke at my fellow PEs who attended that *other* school, University of Michigan). We won Most Active Chapter at the state meeting and our report came in second at the annual NSPE meeting in San Juan, Puerto Rico. (Curious about our competition, I requested a copy of the report submitted by the chapter that won first place . . . and I'm *still* waiting!)

I was subsequently elected to a two-year term as MSPE vice president and served on numerous state-level committees, in particular the political-action committee (PAC). In delivering PAC funds to politicians to help in their reelection campaigns, I learned firsthand what an organization receives in return. Occasionally, I would meet with senators or representatives them-selves, but usually my meetings were with a staff member who listened to our request or issue. The big question on their minds—never spoken—was how many votes we could deliver in the next election or how large a financial contribution we could provide. Once in a while, it appeared that there was sincere interest on their part regarding our issue, but usually I was left with feeling that "they had bigger fish to fry."

Harry Ball, P.E., had become MSPE's executive director in 1976 and was outstanding in serving the members and our profession. (I knew the previous directors, and their performance had been average at best.) Harry had retired from Whirlpool Corp. and took on the MSPE assignment with great vigor and enthusiasm. I concluded that his great success in the assignment came from the fact that he was also one of *us*, a P.E.

During this period, professional engineers, architects, and land surveyors were keenly interested in ensuring the Michigan legislature understood the importance of the licenses we all held and the laws governing licensure. The three professional organizations—Michigan Society of Professional Engineers, American Institute of Architects–Michigan, and Michigan Society of Profes-sional Surveyors—formed the 148 Club, which stood for the 38 senators and 110 representatives in the Michigan legislature. Once a year, at a luncheon for the senators and representatives, society members were asked to host their representative or senator. My representative in District 67 was Debbie Stabenow, and she graciously accepted my invitation for several years. Not only did I get the opportunity to know my representative, I had the privilege of escorting one of the youngest members of the entire legislature. We were always surrounded by a crowd of admirers. As I write this, she will soon be the senior US senator from Michigan. All Michigan citizens are fortunate to have her representing us in the halls of Congress.

. . .

In 1980, we completed the football practice facility that Duffy Daugherty, MSU's winningest football coach, had dreamed about and that which bears his name. Although he left before it was completed, he proudly returned for its dedication on October 5.

The Communication Arts building was completed in 1981, as were the baghouses for boilers 1 and 2 at Power Plant '65. The energy crisis of the early 1970s caused the Communication Arts building to be designed with a special energy-conserving feature. A large water tank was built into the basement where the water was cooled late at night, when the campuswide electrical demand was low. Then, during the day, the building would be cooled by that cold water. At least, that is what was *supposed* to happen. Unfortunately, the tank did not perform up to expectations, as the diaphragm that separated the cooled water from the returning warm water leaked. All attempts to fix it failed, and, reluctantly, it was abandoned.

The Wharton Center for the Performing Arts and its parking ramp were completed in 1983. Finally, MSU had a venue capable of attracting the best shows from Broadway. It remains a "crown jewel" in mid-Michigan.

. . .

Meanwhile, back at the Flinn "ranch" we continued to plant trees. In fact, we were now managing a full-fledged tree farm.

In December 1978, Greg Warfield, a reporter for the *Ingham County News,* contacted Tom Bergeon (my old fellow student employee) and asked to interview him for an article regarding cut-your-own Christmas trees. Tom's parents had established a tree farm many years earlier, and now Tom and his family lived at that farm.

Tom said, "All my trees are really too large. I don't want any more people encouraged to come here. But Flinn, over on Willoughby Road, should have some trees that are large enough to be Christmas trees by this time."

So Greg interviewed me instead. I pointed out that I started planting trees to beautify the acreage. I also thought that I might eventually develop the property as home sites, and trees would certainly make the property more attractive.

A week or two after the story ran, cars were pulling in with customers looking for Christmas trees. Several folks were holding a copy of Greg's newspaper article, saying, "Why don't you advertise? We've been driving up and down Willoughby Road trying to locate you!" I then realized that we were selling an emotional product, and there was a high demand since many of the old cut-your-own farms had gone out of business.

In my desire to quickly cover the property with trees, one year I rented a tree planter from the county conservation office where I also bought my seedlings each year. I ordered 7,000 trees. My old Ferguson TE 20 was not equipped with the remote hydraulic port needed to raise and lower the plow portion of the planter, so I then rented a new Ford tractor from a local dealer. I gave our oldest daughter, Beth, who was 12 years old, a quick lesson in tractor driving.

It had been a very wet spring, and we quickly realized we would get stuck if we tried to plant the low areas. As we were planting a high knoll near the back of the property, nearly a half mile from the house, we got stuck. I walked all the way back to the barn and drove the Ferguson to pull out the stuck Ford. At that point, it began to rain, so I told the kids to jump on the Ferguson and ride back. Then it began to rain harder. Suddenly, we were in the midst of a torrential downpour so strong it shorted out the Ferguson before we reached the barn.

The rain finally stopped at daybreak. I dried off the distributor and wiring harness on the Ferguson, got it restarted, and returned with Beth to pull out the Ford tractor and tree planter. It was now Sunday. I had only rented the Ford for the weekend, and I knew that another tree farm had rented the planter for the following day, Monday. As we were driving back, with just the two of us on the tractor and with no implements attached, on high ground, the rear wheel of the tractor sunk deep into the wet ground, nearly to the axle. This seemed unbelievable, as the fields hadn't been tilled for several years and a heavy layer of turf had become established. Apparently, that didn't matter.

Early Monday morning, I called nearby Andersen Excavating and requested a bulldozer to extract the mired tractors and planter. When it arrived, I told the operator that I was not going to pay more than one day's rental; if he got stuck, it would be his problem. After successfully pulling out all the equipment, he told me, "The dozer nearly went in. I've never seen soil like that!"

So now I'd spent a great deal of money and had planted only a thousand trees. The family could only plant another 3,000 by hand, which meant we still had 3,000 additional trees to get into the ground. That wasn't going to happen. I called the conservation office and told them that if anyone were interested in seedlings, I was willing to give them a good deal. One party that showed up was a Mrs. Snell, along with her daughter and granddaughter. Years earlier, I had taken my kids to the Snell farm, north of Haslett, to cut our own Christmas tree. Mrs. Snell pointed out that her daughter hated planting trees on the farm (as did mine), but now her daughter wanted her daughter to experience planting trees at their cottage up north. (Interestingly, her husband, John Snell, had been chair of Civil Engineering at MSU shortly before I arrived, leaving to form the Snell Engineering firm.) Mrs. Snell's purchase, along with those of some other folks, minimized my loss on the purchase of seedlings.

Other than the ill-fated tree planter scheme, one might assume that this tree-farming business is a low-effort/high-profit enterprise: "Plant 'em and sell 'em!" Right. I admit, I wasn't fully aware of all the work required when I began.

One obvious detail—which somehow escaped my notice at the beginning—is that the rows between trees need to be mowed so customers can easily move about to make their choice. I was surprised how quickly the brush developed. As we kept planting, the amount of mowing needed increased each year. Soon, a walk-behind Gravely Brush Hog was inadequate. Norene said I was spending too many evenings out in the field, mowing. I purchased a small Ford 1210 tractor with a four-foot-wide brush hog, which made life much better.

Then the bugs started. I added a spray rig to the tractor, but it could only carry 50 gallons of spray at a time. So we purchased a hay wagon and a 1,000-gallon water tank so refilling the sprayer didn't require a long trip back to the hydrant at the barn. There's nothing quite like getting into a rubber suit, putting on a respirator, and spending several hot summer days each year spraying trees.

Then there's the shearing. Every pine tree needs to be sheared annually if it's to be a Christmas tree. My son, James, is convinced that one of his arms is longer than the other from shearing all those trees year after year.

After a few years, I understood why all those old tree farms had gone out of business—and why one fellow Michigan tree farmer named his farm "Seldom Rest." (The tree farm provided a unique future opportunity: donating trees to enhance the MSU campus. Numerous Norway spruces and Scotch pines were donated in 1988 and white pines in 2006. I discovered we were in good company when I read Harold Lautner's book, *From an Oak Opening: A Record of the Development of the Campus Park of Michigan State University, 1855–1969*. John Hannah, in the early 1960s, donated trees from his farm, east of Hagadorn Road, now known as Hannah Plaza.)

My early desire to allow my children to experience having a horse was satisfied when my dad, who by then had acquired the Soule farm in New York where I and my siblings were born, was raising horses that were half Arabian. During a visit back east in the early '70s, he took my kids down to his barn and showed them a one-year-old stallion. "This is Blaze," he said, "and he's yours." Dad agreed to have him broke and to send saddle and bridle along with Blaze when he was ready to be delivered.

After Blaze's arrival in East Lansing, I had him gelded, but he was still a lot of horse for a couple of youngsters. Beth wasn't much interested. Lisa worked with him a lot, then lost interest. James finally decided it was okay to sell Blaze to a woman from Charlotte, a few miles southwest of us, who was putting together a riding academy. Neighbors in the subdivision backing up to our property were upset with Blaze leaving, as they would no longer be able to look out their back windows and see this beautiful animal prancing around in the pasture with his tail up, as Arabians do.

I can truly say, "I had a one-horse operation, and I shut that down!"

■　■　■

Ted Simon turned 65 on September 15, 1982, and began to talk seriously of retirement. I thought MSU should acknowledge his significant contributions to the university by renaming the power plant in his honor.

A bit of background: During the 1950s, the State of Michigan told Consumers Power (now Consumers Energy) and Detroit Edison, two leading power providers, to expand their electrical-generating capacities as the state was expected to grow rapidly. When MSU realized it would also need more steam-heating capacity, Ted and our consulting engineers—Benjamin, Woodhouse, & Gunther—recommended continuing the cogeneration of electricity

The Clifton and Dolores Wharton Center for the Performing Arts was completed in 1982. This photo also shows the new front addition completed in 2009.

that existed in the Shaw Lane and old North Campus plants. Consumers Power was incensed; they viewed the state's authorization and funding of electrical generation—rather than purchasing power from them—a violation of the agreement that had led them to invest heavily in expanding their own power plants. Consumers Power had much support in the legislature, and the fight was on. Finally, the legislature sought an independent opinion and hired the A. M. Kinney company of Cincinnati, Ohio. Their September 1963 report stated, "After careful analysis of the estimated investment and operating costs for all plans considered, the Engineers recommend the immediate adoption of Plan 1: Full electric-power generation." Thus, lawmakers approved proceeding with MSU's plan.

President Hannah's efforts, for the most part, focused on obtaining approval and funding from the Michigan legislature for MSU's annual budget request. In other words, the last thing he wanted was "ruffled feathers" in state government. He told Ted, "I hope your winning this battle doesn't cause us to lose the war." Ted didn't say anything, but it was obvious that it hurt for our iconic president to suggest he may have injured MSU. Later, during the early 1970s and subsequent energy crisis, Ted's wisdom was acknowledged by many companies and individuals across the country, as we had the correct answer regarding fuel availability and overall efficiency. So, in late 1982, I wrote a letter to Jack Breslin, with Roger Wilkinson's concurrence, stating:

> MSU's 1980–81 energy costs were $11,400,000, while the University of Michigan expended $23,250,000 to supply nearly the same building square footage.
>
> Ted Simon has been instrumental in planning, promoting, and constructing the original plant and all subsequent additions. His insistence, during his 36 years at MSU, that all new buildings and systems be as energy efficient as possible, contributed in no small measure to this success story. One could easily say that through his leadership and foresight, MSU enjoys nearly a $12,000,000 annual endowment, which will continue to benefit the institution as long as cogeneration of steam and electricity and prudent energy utilization are maintained.
>
> As you know, Ted has strongly indicated his plan to retire this year, and once he officially announces his retirement date, I recommend MSU rename Power Plant '65 to "Theodore B. Simon Cogenerating Power Station" in recognition of his dedication to the institution and the continuing financial benefit it enjoys.

Today, the former Power Plant '65 is known as the T. B. Simon Power Plant.

Ted identified February 1984 as his retirement date, and my game plan was to become successful in replacing him as assistant vice president for Physical Plant.

Success

knew the campaign to replace Ted Simon as assistant vice president for Physical Plant was going to be very challenging and a real "horse race." There were some hard feelings toward Physical Plant across campus. Since I had been there for more than 20 years, some folks thought I was part of the problem, not a solution.

One day, several of the old guard from the shops asked if I wasn't upset with the university for conducting a nationwide search for Ted's replacement after all I'd done to get prepared. I replied, "No, the campus needs to get the best person possible. I think I know who that is, but I may be wearing rose-colored glasses." And then I said, "I realize it's 1984: If a person of color or a female with my credentials applies, I'll have a new boss. But I also know there are many other employers willing to pay such candidates much more than MSU plans to pay."

As my competitors came to campus for interviews, I was able to learn who they were by perusing the guest book at the power plant, as all visitors are required to sign in. Norm Bedell from Duke University was the first to visit. I was told later that he was the only candidate, other than me, with hands-on power plant experience. After returning to Duke, though, he withdrew his application.

My experience in interviewing with Eastern Michigan, Notre Dame, and the University of Illinois served me well when it was my turn to meet with the interview committee. They asked the normal questions, i.e., "Why do you want this job?" When they asked, "What will you do, that's different, in the first 90 days?" I said, "I will meet with the deans, one on one." This highlighted how my approach would differ from Ted's; he saw no reason to meet with the deans, since he got a clear message from Karl McDonel, secretary of the Board of Trustees, that he was above them when he was appointed Superintendent of Buildings and Utilities in 1956.

I was appointed assistant vice president (AVP) on July 1, 1984, reporting directly to Vice President Roger Wilkinson, who said, "You don't fully appreciate what you pulled off!" He repeated that statement for several months. I eventually learned that Provost Lee Winder had once adamantly stated, "When that Ted Simon retires, there's going to be a new face over there." (There was no love lost between the two of them.) The positive relationships I had established over the years with members of the faculty—some of whom became members of the interview committee, such as Dean Von Tersch—were key to my overcoming the provost's mandate.

Two years later, after visiting my son, who was in the US Marine Corps and stationed in Beaufort, South Carolina, I decided to stop at Duke University on my way home and determine why Norm Bedell had withdrawn his application. During our conversation, I joked, "I thought it was a good thing the interview was during winter, causing a southern boy like you to decide not to come to the Snow Belt."

Norm laughed and said, "I'm a native of Gaylord, Michigan, and I earned my first degree at MSU while living in Snyder-Phillips Hall for four years. No, the reason I withdrew was as soon as I was picked up at the airport by the chair of the committee, John Lewis, all I heard were alleged problems regarding Physical Plant. The next day, meeting with various campus groups, such as Housing and Food Services, I heard the same message. I wasn't willing to come to a campus where the feelings were so negative toward Physical Plant." This reinforced my conviction to improve the division's customer relations, which was already underway.

Almost immediately, upon my becoming the AVP, Ted Simon's secretary, Dorlene Bayhan, reminded me that she had originally hired into B&U to be the assistant to Ralph Bremer, who headed the Business Office. When Ted's secretary at that time left to get married, Ted told Dorlene he wanted her to become his secretary, and she was afraid to say no. (During the 1950s, one was always reluctant to disagree with the Big Boss, and Ted possessed an intimidating persona.) She had remained with him for years, but now she saw an opportunity to finally make a change. "Are you telling me that you would rather return to working in the Business Office than work for me?" I asked. She said yes. I approved the transfer and considered how best to fill the position.

Keith Groty, AVP for Personnel and Employee Relations, suggested I promote someone who appeared to have potential. Donna Irish, who was my administrative assistant when I was in charge of Engineering Services and an obvious choice, preferred to stay in Engineering. But she recommended Deborah Dohm, who had recently transferred from Housing and Food Services. With some reservation, Deborah agreed to "give it a try." (I really tried not to take all the rejections and reluctance too personally.) Deborah has handled the assignment extremely well, and her personality helps reinforce the open-door policy that was greatly needed. She continues serving in that role today, working for my successor.

Meeting with deans was step one in addressing our customer service problem; many other steps were needed to improve staff morale and build team spirit. I detailed these efforts in my paper "Improving Customer Relations, Even During Rough Times," which I presented at the 75th anniversary meeting of APPA in Washington, DC, on July 25, 1988.

In July 1984, I became the assistant vice president for physical plant at Michigan State University. During the six-month selection process, and the various interviews and meetings with the screening committee, vice presidents, provosts, etc., I was repeatedly told the Physical Plant Division had a serious customer relations problem. The first step taken to address this was to meet with each dean and key director, one-on-one. We are a very large campus with 15 colleges, as well as several other key programs and departments, including the library. The meetings with the deans revealed the following perceptions:

The Physical Plant
- has a low level of productivity, and is slow to get a job done,
- costs are too high,

- tends to be uncommunicative,
- becomes defensive when costs are challenged or inquiries are made,
- is inflexible, and
- customer work appears to receive very low priority.

Taking all of this input under advisement, and accepting the tenet that a perceived problem is a problem indeed, I set about analyzing how a team who had put together one of the finest set of facilities, operated at one of the lowest costs in the country, could acquire such a poor image. . . .

I set about determining if the various perceptions had any foundation. On the issue of poor communication, I found that our staff would frequently state, "I'm so busy, I didn't have a chance to get back to that customer." We had, on occasion, responded with a firm letter after receiving a critical note from across campus. I discovered there was definitely a misconception of what we are funded for, and when we turned down a request as being an item we're not funded for, we were tagged as being inflexible. This situation was exacerbated with the service reductions caused by the severe budget cuts. In reviewing the large number of customer jobs, one had to admit that the delayed completion times revealed that the projects were not our highest priority.

The meetings with the deans were an unqualified success. Several had their key associates with them in the meetings, and once it became obvious that I wasn't attempting to defend any past actions, and that I was genuinely interested in improving relations, they frequently ended by complementing our service, expressing sympathy with our budget cuts, and pointing out exemplary Physical Plant employees they knew and had observed. I concluded these sessions with an offer to bring my managers to a meeting with the deans and his/her chairs so they could "meet their Physical Plant." Several took us up on our offer, and the meetings were friendly, although most contained periods of spirited and sharp comments regarding past service delivery problems. All meetings ended on a very cordial note, and we were given high marks for adopting the posture, "Since we don't pay taxes or make a profit, and our staff is paid less than contractors' employees, our costs should be lower than any contractor," and we intend to be "helpers, not hinders." An instrument I found invaluable in these meetings was what we refer to as the Dean's Booklet. This collection of documents was extremely effective in answering a myriad of questions. The booklet contains:

- *A Classification of Accounts for Physical Plant—APPA.* This document has been very effective in answering the question, "Is there a national guideline which recommends what services a physical plant division is funded for?"
- *MSU-Funded Responsibilities.* MSU's Physical Plant, like all other major universities, has unique, and in certain cases, peculiar funded responsibilities. This instrument explains those, as well as provides a more detailed explanation than the APPA document.
- *Budget Reductions.* This section of the briefing book details the substantial reductions in Physical Plant services required as a result of budget reductions during the '80s. Alone, or as part of the briefing book, this section has substantially reduced complaints from administrators who have forgotten—or never knew—about service reductions implemented to meet drastic revenue decreases in the first half of the decade. . . .
- *Big Ten Physical Plant Unit Cost Data.* Top administrators are often concerned with comparative data. . . . This section of the briefing book, a single sheet, compares Michigan State to the other Big Ten institutions; sister institutions in terms of mission, programs, location, climate, labor force characteristics, and—generally—size of the campuses and student bodies.
- *Grant Overhead.* Many researchers complained about having to pay for repairs on research equipment since they had a misconception regarding the disbursement of overhead dollars. This document clarifies the issue by showing that the Physical Plant only received the funds to support the "normally funded" services.
- *Facts about Construction Costs.* Very effective in disproving the cliché, "Physical Plant is too expensive!"
- *Annual Report.* By enclosing the most recent copy of the Annual Report in the Dean's Booklet, the newly arrived deans are quickly informed of the division's current status.
- *Energy Programs.* Developed in 1980, near the height of national public concern about energy resources and also at the beginning of Michigan State's financial straits, this booklet outlines a Michigan State history of energy conservation. Its inclusion in the briefing book for deans, department heads, and other officials promotes an understanding of Michigan State's long role in prudent energy management.

An additional step was to reestablish a true alterations and improvement crew in our skilled trades shop, whose mission was to compete with the local contractors as to cost and swiftness of completion. They have been successful to the point where we now have campus customers preferring to wait for our alterations and improvement crew, rather than have us call in a contractor on open order. Quite frankly, we had to realize that we moved too slowly in modifying our organization to match the increasing load of customer-paid work during the past two decades. This organizational change, along with our willingness to go out and meet with the campus customer, has created an environment where we seldom receive a critical note. Phone calls of concern start with, "I realize your difficult budget situation . . ."

During various meetings, and after a review of customer complaints, it became obvious that we had a fair number of employees in Physical Plant who had marginal people skills, and some of whom seemed to delight in creating poor images and examples to confirm that we were truly guilty of the allegations. Correcting this type of behavior is, quite frankly, more of a challenge than to deal directly with the customer on a particular issue. It's also an extreme high priority, in that one bad incident can undo several years of hard work in image building. In 1981, I agreed to divorce myself from the daily engineering and construction responsibilities and take on the challenge of our custodial, maintenance, and alterations. . . .

The first step I took was to take the time to meet the folks in their building and during their shift. I was frequently told, "You know, you're the only director who has ever come out to meet us."

The second step was to convince the work force that it was a "new day," and that lack of proper performance would be addressed appropriately and not be ignored. This firm but fair approach includes an annual performance rating of each employee by his/her supervisor which I personally review. In this way, I am able to better know my staff members and to assess the uniformity of the ratings being performed. This firm but fair approach has caused many individuals to leave our division; some voluntarily and others at the end of the disciplinary chain. The only "bad apples" that remain have modified their actions so their performance is at least satisfactory.

The third step was to establish an annual custodial training session. The Manager, at times, invited the president to come over to meet all of our custodians. This outing fostered, "If the president of the university comes over to meet you, you are an important person!" These sessions, as well as an annual Christmas party held in the Physical Plant Building, have helped to dispel the feeling of alienation on the part of custodians who punch in at their own building and don't have a close physical kinship with the Physical Plant Division. Subsequently, the president has also met with our skilled trades maintenance and alterations team.

The fourth step was to establish a quality quarterly newsletter to provide the recognition of our achievers. This newsletter is favorably received by our employees, and our editor is swamped with articles. It's no accident that there is not a column from the assistant vice president. [I was convinced our tradesmen, and others, would view such a column as propaganda from upper management. The newsletter needed to be theirs, not mine.]

During meetings with employees, I became aware the folks in the Electric Shop didn't know the folks in the Plumbing Shop, even though the shops are adjacent to one another. This problem was significantly improved by building a quality photo gallery of our entire division and mounting it on our lunchroom wall with a special section for retirees and another for new employees. This has been effective in our folks becoming acquainted and has helped create a stronger team attitude. The photo gallery also assists in recognizing our achievers as decals are affixed to the photos of newly promoted employees.

A unique morale problem which existed with our skilled trades group (their rate of pay being significantly lower than the outside construction trades) was solved by establishing a higher paying classification: "Master Mechanic." We not only were able to raise the pay, but the individuals feel a sense of accomplishment since they must pass an examination in their trade area to be promoted.

It's my assessment that one must know one's teammates if you're going to build team spirit, and I feel it is essential to meet each new full-time employee when they come on board and each employee who is promoted. (These folks must be our superstars if we're promoting them!) I ask the first line supervisor to accompany these folks, and the conversation frequently touches on the importance of our mission in serving the institution. (I frequently mention the Carnegie Foundation poll, which found a majority of students select a college on the appearance of the buildings and grounds.)

It has become obvious that part of the training program for our employees

The Indoor Tennis Facility was completed in 1986, North of Jolly Road and across the street from the Forest Akers West Golf Course.

PHOTO COURTESY OF MSU COMMUNICATIONS AND BRAND STRATEGY.

needs to include coaching in order to better equip them to communicate with our campus customer. Our supervisors must be coaches, and bringing them together in quarterly meetings has been an effective step in developing uniform approach and attitude. In addition, we have found it effective to include in these meetings the nonsupervisory personnel who also have frequent customer contact, such as secretaries, communication clerks, engineers, architects, and estimators; we call the larger group the Management Team. The Dale Carnegie course has been the most effective formal training session for our people, and we now offer these folks the opportunity to attend at divisional expense.

I am convinced the above steps have been instrumental in improving our image and performance; our absenteeism has fallen, the number of grievances is down, and critical letters and reports from across campus are rare. I take the position that each employee is the ambassador of the entire division when they contact a campus customer, and the impression left by that individual is the image of our entire division, including myself. If they're not successful,

I'm not successful. Therefore, my most difficult mission is to get to know each of our 500 employees on a first-name basis.

■   ■   ■

During 1984–85, the tennis facility was built north of Mount Hope Road, a new Dairy Barn was added to the Dairy Center on College Road, and major additions were built onto Plant Biology and the Duffy Daugherty building.

John DiBiaggio replaced Cecil Mackey as president of MSU on July 1, 1985.

Jack Breslin turned 65 during July 1985, and the university policy at that time required administrators to retire at that age. John DiBiaggio wisely asked Jack to stay on as the university's liaison to the state legislature. The bulk of his former duties were transferred to Vice President for Finance and Operations Roger Wilkinson.

We moved into the second half of the 1980s with a new president and a hope that Michigan's economic situation would improve and provide some relief for the facilities' budgets.

New Challenges

A s I assumed the AVP position on July 1, 1984, it was necessary to fill certain key positions, and MSU was fortunate to have existing staff members who had grown and developed the leadership skills needed, including Bob Nestle (Engineering Services), Terry Ruprecht (Maintenance and Utility Distribution), Joe Kavanagh (Power and Water), and Gene Garrison (Automotive Services). Dr. Roy Simon had joined the Physical Plant division several months earlier as director of Telecommunication Services, reporting to Terry Ruprecht.

In December, Melvin Latnie joined us as the manager of Custodial Services. When the custodial supervisors learned he was black, I was told there was apprehension and concern. Within two weeks of his arrival, however, most reported, "He's the best person I've ever worked for." Mel was instrumental in dramatically improving the morale in his department.

One day, George Leroi, chair of Chemistry and soon-to-be dean of the College of Natural Science, telephoned me and asked, "Ron, couldn't you use a mechanical engineer?" Mechanical engineers with HVAC experience are not easy to find. I agreed to meet with George and his candidate, Phuong Nguyen. Phuong and his family were so-called boat people who had fled Vietnam and been "adopted" by George's church. Phuong joined Engineering Services early in 1984, helping to confirm MSU's commitment to diversity. (Phuong is now a senior mechanical engineer at the cyclotron.)

Environmental regulations continued to tighten. We developed programs to address asbestos abatement, removal of underground storage tanks, and removal of PCBs.

Regrettably, the budget situation did not improve, and it was a rare year that didn't bring an additional budget cut. MSU's budget situation was known by many other institutions, and so, in 1987, Joe Estill, with Texas A&M, asked me to serve on an Experience Exchange panel with him and Craig Roloff, from Montana State, and present "Managing in Hard Times" at the International APPA meeting in New Orleans. Joe asked me to present my story first. After I finished my comments and answered questions, I turned the podium back to Joe. He had a strange look on his face. He said, "Craig and I thought *we* had taken budget cuts. But your experience has eclipsed anything we've dealt with. We have nothing to add." Later that year, the severity of the budget situation was dramatized by MSU deciding to defer repairs to the iconic clock and carillon at Beaumont Tower, causing the chimes to cease ringing on the hour and quarter hour.

Norene and I decided to attend the 1988 Rose Bowl in support of MSU's football team. We had a great time, as Coach Perles and the Spartans won. We had elected not to go in 1966, and after this long "drought," we were so proud of our team and university that we immediately joined the Alumni Association as Life Members.

Just a month later, a campus accident brought national attention to an athletic facility under construction. As the erection crew was moving the second set of huge roof trusses into position on the structural ring beam of the Breslin Center, the trusses fell, causing the two large crane booms to be bent over the ring beam. The cranes were actually lifted off the ground and slammed back down so violently that the very heavy counterweights on the back of the crane bodies fell off. Fortunately, nether crane operator sustained major injuries. This construction accident made national news and gave the Physical Plant team experience in dealing with the media's demand for more and more information over an extended period of time. Unfortunately, Jack Breslin himself was a witness to this event, watching from his office window. (We lost Jack to terminal bone cancer later that year, on August 2.)

During 1988, the director position at the University of Illinois was open once again. This time, they were successful in recruiting an MSU candidate, although it was not me: Terry Ruprecht accepted the position.

■　■　■

During the summer of '88, it appeared that the Clerical Technical Union (CTU) was considering a September strike, believing that the fall-term student registration would fail if they were not working. The CTU contract had expired March 31, and the union's negotiating team refused to budge from its demand for a very high wage increase. On July 19, Provost David Scott and Vice President Roger Wilkinson established an ad hoc committee (Work Interruption Contingency Planning) to develop a contingency plan. The main goals were to accomplish fall-term registration and maintain security, communications, delivery of materials, refuse disposal, and feeding of animals. Three subcommittees were identified: communications, registration, and security. The real surprise came when I was asked to chair the committee.

As I was walking out of the meeting room with Keith Groty, I inquired, "Just how the hell does the *facility* guy get tagged with this assignment?!"

Keith quietly replied, "Ron, they want to make sure this effort is successful."

I still thought it was an odd arrangement, but I probably should have viewed it as a compliment or endorsement of my managerial abilities.

Needless to say, the committee, along with wide support from the campus community, successfully accomplished all its goals, even though the CTU was on strike from September 13 to 28.

■　■　■

Since 1929, MSU's North Campus has had unique lanterns lighting the walkways. Many folks think they may be the third most recognizable symbol at MSU, after Beaumont Tower and the Spartan statue.

During the early 1970s, when concerns about adequate lighting at night were raised by the campus community, it was suggested that we supplement the lanterns with a different style of fixture (mushroom fixtures) to increase the overall lumen level. Instead, I asked the electric shop to replace the lanterns' incandescent bulbs with mercury vapor bulbs, which greatly increased the lumen level and eliminated the need for additional fixtures. I was then criticized for "ruining the campus ambiance." But given the deteriorating condition of the lanterns themselves, it was a temporary solution at best.

The lanterns were constructed with a thin copper frame, a glass lens held in place by small clips, and a door to access the bulb. Thus, the lanterns were a bit fragile, and many had been vandalized by snowballs and hockey sticks over the years. We discovered that the iron lampposts had deteriorated as well.

In the late 1980s, we mounted a campaign to save the lanterns. Our creative sheet-metal team developed a prototype fixture that replicated the original fixtures but used ¼-inch copper plate (in place of the thin frame), with access to the bulb through the bottom of the fixture. The lens is a tube of Lexan, nearly unbreakable, which reinforces the copper frame. The replacement lampposts were constructed from fiberglass colored with a copper patina, making any future chipping virtually invisible. The new posts raised the lanterns two feet higher to help keep them out of harm's way. The new lanterns were equipped with sodium vapor bulbs, which provide even more lumens but produce a soft yellow glow and enhanced ambiance.

We were about to proceed with replacing the lanterns when, in a weekly vice president's meeting, Roger Wilkinson asked, "What are you going to do with the old ones?"

Remembering Vince Vandenburg's story—"No one should have one"—I said, "We will crush them."

Assistant Vice President for Finance Steve Terry spoke up and said, "But I've always wanted one!"

I thought, *Uh oh, it could be quite a challenge to make them available to any and all interested parties in a fair manner.*

The only acceptable approach was to hold an auction after widespread notification had been issued. The Alumni Office notified alumni via its magazine, and the campus *News-Bulletin* and *State News* spread the word. My telephone started to ring with messages. I asked Deborah Dohm to handle and document the flood of calls we received. A number of her conversations went something like this:

CALLER: "I need the fixture located southwest of Mary Mayo Hall. I met my wife under that lantern."
RESPONSE: "You'll need to come to the auction on October 21, 1989, which is also Homecoming Weekend."

Farm Lane Bridge with lanterns. Shaw Hall, in the background, confirms the photo was taken after 1950.

CALLER: "I can't. I live in California and my business makes it impossible for me to attend the auction."

RESPONSE: "You could give us a proxy bid, and we will submit it on your behalf during the auction."

CALLER: "How much will it cost?"

RESPONSE: "We don't know. It's an *auction*. You'll have to decide how much you're willing to pay."

Numerous proxy bids were authorized and some were successful. The old fixtures were laid out on hay wagons borrowed from the MSU farms and moved into the Judging Pavilion, located south of the International Center. Bill Sheridan from Mason, Michigan, volunteered to be the auctioneer. (Sheridan was inducted into the National Auctioneers Hall of Fame in 2014.)

The auction raised nearly $25,000, which was placed in an account to fund future maintenance of the lanterns.

■　■　■

Several major structures were built during the late 1980s, including the Plant and Soil Science building, the Engineering Research complex, the Kellogg Center parking ramp, and Engineering Addition 2, as well as the Breslin Center. This increased building space placed additional stress on the Simon Power Plant's ability to produce steam during the heating season. As additional buildings were built, the potential for a catastrophic outage increased. By 1985, we recognized the need to increase the steam generating capacity.

In February 1986, I sent a letter to Jack Breslin, with copies to Roger Wilkinson and Provost Lee Winder, stating, "As you know, the only source of heating steam for the MSU campus is the T. B. Simon Power Plant, which also cogenerates 98% of the university's electricity. The original boilers 1 & 2 are now 20 years old. . . . Equipment of this age will experience increased unscheduled outages. As a consequence, the campus is increasingly vulnerable to forced outages during peak heating periods, which will inflict severe damage to research and cause significant disruption to the educational environment. . . . The most cost-effective solution is to immediately proceed with a new 350,000 lb/hr steam generator at an estimated cost of $37,400,000."

Numerous meetings took place with representatives from various levels of state government. In a December 1987 memorandum, Mel McClung, of the Department of Management and Budget, said, "Mr. Naftaly, State of Michigan budget director, recognizes MSU's need for this power plant. . . . A way needs to be found to finance it."

In June 1988, Joe Kavanagh received the permit to install boiler 4 from the Department of Natural Resources. Michigan's Joint Capital Outlay Committee released $100,000 for the preparation of preliminary plans. At their meeting on July 30, 1988, the MSU Board of Trustees appointed Black and Veatch as engineer/architect for the Unit 4 addition.

Black and Veatch completed the preliminary design phase in January 1989. They recommended Unit 4 also include a 16.5-megawatt, steam-driven turbine electrical generator. Delays in proceeding and inflation pushed the estimated project cost to $61,500,000.

Gordon Guyer, who replaced Jack Breslin as VP for Governmental Affairs,

The Jack Breslin Student Events Center completed in 1989, shown here with the Berkowitz Addition that provided practice gymnasiums for basketball as well as enhanced offices for both basketball coaches.

and I met with Senator John Engler during May 1989 to discuss the project. Engler asked, "Why are you asking the State of Michigan to fund this project when there is plenty of private money and interest for such projects?" It was obvious: Engler was very much opposed to the State funding Unit 4. Even though the State of Michigan had funded all previous power plant projects, Gordon and I agreed to explore potential funding from private entities.

Two other universities, Western Michigan and Saginaw Valley State, had also requested funding for power-related projects, causing the Joint Capital Outlay Committee to hire two consulting firms—Giffels Hoyem/Basso and Miller, Canfield, Paddock, & Stone—to make a comparative cost analysis of university ownership versus purchasing power. Lansing Board of Water and Light and Consumers Energy each submitted proposals regarding MSU's challenge. After reviewing the proposals, the consultants, on March 9, 1990, concluded, "There is no indication that the State would benefit from accepting any of the utilities' proposals."

During this period, when factions in the legislature were questioning the importance of Unit 4, I received a call from a key member of the House or Senate Fiscal Agency asking for a tour of the power plant ASAP. I met him at the plant that day. Following our tour, he said, "I still wonder why you're so adamant that this is the right thing to do."

I replied, "MSU's annual energy bill is $25,000,000 lower than U of M. That makes Unit 4 a three-year payback."

"I'm surprised you know the U of M numbers," he said as he walked out. The University of Michigan was known for not publicly sharing such information, but I considered it my job to know the numbers.

The Joint Capital Outlay Committee unanimously approved proceeding with Unit 4 at their April 10 meeting. Even so, there were those in government who still believed it was the wrong thing to do—especially Senator Engler, who, a few months later, became the Republican candidate for governor, facing incumbent Jim Blanchard in the November election. Engler's chance of winning seemed very slim.

Gerry Mills was a recently retired captain with the Lansing Police Department who agreed to run on the Republican ticket for the vacant House seat in District 67. Coincidently, at that time Norene was volunteering at Ingham Medical Center and her partner volunteer was Gerry's wife, Patti. One day in late summer, Norene said to me, "We need to attend a meeting tomorrow night to support Gerry." Well, I knew what that meant: "Get out the checkbook!"

When we arrived at the event, I realized all the top Republicans were in attendance. The buzz in the room was that Engler might also attend. Sure enough, after a large sedan pulled up outside, the door to the room swung open, and Engler's press secretary, John Truscott, marched in with a boom box on his shoulder, blasting Engler's newly minted campaign song.

Two years earlier, John had been a student employee in the Physical Plant business office, so we knew each other. Our greeting each other as old friends was not lost on Engler. When he finally approached me, and both of us knowing his chances of winning were slim, I decided to appear optimistic and supportive. I said, "*Governor,* the two consultants have submitted their reports recommending proceeding with Unit 4, and we're ready to proceed." He just nodded and moved on.

A couple of weeks later, Steve Webster, a staff member in Gordon Guyer's office, called and said, "Engler has gone silent on your power plant project and no one knows why." Steve had come to MSU in 1987 after serving in the House Fiscal Agency and was very connected within the legislature.

Governor Blanchard signed the Capital Outlay Bill on October 12, 1990, which allowed MSU to authorize Black and Veatch to begin designing Unit 4.

The MSU Board of Trustees awarded contracts for the long lead time components—the boiler and turbine generator, totaling $24,000,000—at their November 30, 1990, meeting.

Around February 1, 1991, just after Governor Engler took office following his surprising win, I was asked by Steve Webster, "What would be the impact if the project were canceled?"

I said, "The boiler and turbine generator vendors would insist on receiving their expected profits." I then reminded him of how critical this facility was for the mission of the university. A few days later I was told, "Keep going. The project is too far along to cancel."

I'm convinced that Norene's insistence that we support Gerry Mill's campaign was a big factor in slowing resistance to the Unit 4 project at a crucial time.

■　■　■

During the 1980s, I continued to be active in my professional organizations, after serving two terms (four years) as a vice president in MSPE, I was elected president for 1989–90. I was a member of the APPA Energy Task Force for three years and was its chair in 1989.

Bill Middleton became APPA's president in 1990–91 and needed to reduce his teaching load at the APPA Institute. He asked me to take on the customer service class. I knew that if I were ever asked I would have to agree, given how important my own experience had been at the 1967 NAPPA Workshop. I ended up teaching for seven years.

When I became the AVP for Physical Plant, AVP for Housing and Food Services Bob Underwood offered to sponsor me for membership in the Rotary Club of Lansing. For many years, Ted Simon and Emery Foster, former AVP for Housing and Food Services, both belonged to the Rotary Club of Lansing and John Hannah had been its president in 1939–40. I accepted. I'm very pleased to be a member of an organization that vigorously attempts to eradicate polio worldwide. I had a good friend in Buffalo whose spine was twisted into an *S* shape by polio, causing her height to be shortened approximately 18 inches. She spent two years in an iron lung. I was hugely relieved that the polio vaccine was available by the time my own children were born.

R³ and Radiation

D avid Scott became provost in 1986 and was a driving force in shaping the university's budgets. His "R³: Refocusing, Rebalancing, and Refining" program forecasted additional budget cuts for Physical Plant services, causing us to issue the following guidelines to prioritize service responsibilities:

- Maintain security and safety systems (door locks, hinges, fire alarms, etc.);
- assure reliability of utility systems (heat, electricity, water, gas, and communications);
- satisfy codes, laws, and regulations regarding operations, safety, and sanitation;
- keep weather out of buildings; maintain roofs, exterior walls, windows, and doors;
- avoid reduction of services that would cause property loss; maintain exterior paint, floor finishes, water treatment, fire sprinklers, etc.;
- maintain energy consuming systems to avoid waste;

- maintain minimum occupant comfort and convenience (elevators, air conditioning, etc.); and
- keep up the appearance of the "campus front door"; entrance lobbies and first floor corridors have priority.

The document had attachments itemizing services already eliminated—interior painting, window washing, etc.—and reduced. It also pointed out the detrimental impact of additional budget cuts. It ended with this request: "We would appreciate ideas on how best to face the financial dilemma without irrevocably harming the University's mission."

On a brighter note, it was recognized that MSU had not adequately funded for utility extensions and replacement. In discussions with David Scott, Roger Wilkinson, and Associate Provost Lou Anna Simon, it was agreed that reliability of the power plant and utility distribution systems was of paramount importance; any remaining funds in the fuel account at year's end would remain with the Physical Plant. In future years, we were able to increase the funds to better address these essential needs.

In February 1990, the University Architects Office became part of Physical Plant. This was the first step in consolidating facilities planning, design, and construction.

■ ■ ■

President John DiBiaggio delighted in informing assembled groups at Cowles House, if I were in attendance, that I was responsible for his being negatively written up in the media.

There was an awning on the back of Cowles House that covered only a small portion of the deck. DiBiaggio wanted a much bigger awning to make the deck more useable, especially on hot, sunny days or when it rained. I pointed out that John Hannah wouldn't even air condition the house for fear of how the media might write it up. But DiBiaggio said, "Ron, you know this building is really a reception center and a big tool to support fund raising." I agreed and, with his directive, had the awning replaced. He asked for the media to be invited for the unveiling; his wife, Nancy, waited at the front door to greet them. However, reporters instead snuck over the back fence, took photos of the awning, and ran stories with headlines that essentially read: "John DiBiaggio feathers his own nest."

■ ■ ■

In early February 1991, a plaster ceiling in a ground-floor corridor of Morrill Hall fell without warning. This certainly shocked the building's occupants and further confirmed the belief that Morrill Hall, which was built with a timber frame and flooring in 1900, was reaching the end of its useful life.

This event also helped spur the upper administration to review the condition of other university facilities and properties. They found deteriorated classrooms, libraries, and laboratories, as well as a campus park in need of attention. It was also noted that research efforts were being attempted in spaces in Giltner Hall and Fee Hall, which had antiquated and/or inadequate facilities. An estimated $189 million was needed to address the situation. At the same time the campus was in great need of a fiber-optic cable network connecting all major buildings.

The State of Michigan didn't step up to the challenge, which led to tuition increases. The available funds never reached the estimated level of need, so we had to take creative steps. For example, we installed fiber-optic cable in the steam tunnels rather than construct additional communication-duct banks (buried conduits encased in concrete that carried telephone wires, coaxial cables, etc.), which would have been very expensive.

During 1991–92, members of the Board of Trustees agreed it would be a good idea to take a tour of certain buildings that the administration identified as needing major repairs. When the tour took place, only Trustee Reinhold (now Foster) showed up. She agreed with the recommendations, and this resulted in an infrastructure/technology fee of $25 per semester starting spring semester 1993. We hoped this would be the first step in building an adequate fund to address deferred maintenance, but, unfortunately, it never grew.

■ ■ ■

Fred Poston became dean of the College of Agriculture and Natural Resources in 1991, just in time to guide the "Revitalization of Michigan Agriculture" program, which was beginning to gain support from the State of Michigan.

Gordon Guyer replaced John DiBiaggio as MSU president on September 1, 1992, just as the campus moved from the quarter system to semesters.

Also in September, a major electrical failure occurred at the Simon Power Plant. A high-voltage transformer on the north side of the building exploded, releasing a large quantity of PCB-laden oil. It was feared that the spill may have reached the river, as some fluid had entered the storm sewer. Fortunately, it did not. Nevertheless, the cleanup and restoration took months and were exceedingly expensive, approaching $2 million. (The most-contaminated soil ended up being loaded onto railroad cars for disposal in Utah.) It became obvious that all high-voltage connections must routinely be unwrapped and carefully inspected for corrosion.

After Gordon Guyer moved into Cowles House, he asked that the front steps be removed and the entrance made wheelchair accessible. We thought it could be accomplished during the next year, but the president said, "I want to be able to drag my Christmas tree up the slope this December!" This caused the project to be declared "critical and top priority." With great collaboration and cooperation between members of Physical Plant, Campus Park and Planning, and Clark Construction Co., the deed was accomplished. (When it came time to do the masonry work, Clark Construction suggested we use Bob Brunger from our own Physical Plant shop, since "he's the best mason in the area.")

■　■　■

The APPA organization has 6 chapters in the United States, and the State of Michigan along with 6 other Midwestern states comprise the Midwest Region of APPA (MAPPA).

In the fall of 1991, MAPPA held its annual meeting in St. Paul, Minnesota, and I became its president. During the discussion regarding future meetings, whose location rotates through the member states, it was noted that 1993 would be Michigan's turn. I knew MSU had never hosted, so we were tagged.

My first step upon returning to campus was to call the Kellogg Center and reserve as many rooms as possible. The second call was to the president's office to schedule the welcoming address. I thought it would be delivered by DiBiaggio, but then Guyer became president in '92, and he was scheduled. But Peter McPherson became president two days before our conference began; he delivered the welcoming address. From time to time, I would remind Peter that I was the first person at MSU to put him to work!

Peter actually came to MSU a month earlier and wanted to meet key administrative personnel. When I entered the room, expecting a greeting such as "you must be Flinn," he actually said, "How the hell did you get the State of Michigan to fund that power plant addition?!"

When I got my wits about me, I said, "It must have been the best answer for all parties or else it wouldn't have happened." (Peter's brusque question was additional confirmation that our winning Unit 4 was an exceptional accomplishment.)

■ ■ ■

In January 1993, while teaching at the APPA Institute, I noticed a small bump under my right jaw. During my annual physical in early summer, I pointed out the bump to Dr. John Strandmark, our family physician. He gave me the names of two head-and-neck surgeons he recommended, and I chose Dr. Kurt Richardson, as he had installed an ear tube for me a couple of years earlier.

After his initial examination, Dr. Richardson suggested taking a biopsy. (He said it would hurt, and it did.) The pathology report was inconclusive. To be safe, he recommended removing the submandibular gland. On September 8, I had the surgery. When I awoke, Dr. Richardson was distraught. He said, "Since the biopsy was inconclusive and most bumps on salivary glands are benign, I didn't discuss with you what should happen if the bump turned out to be something serious. But it is. It is adenoid cystic carcinoma. I know we should go back into surgery and I should take more tissue. But that will leave half of your tongue numb for life, and the right corner of your mouth will droop. This is such an uncommon cancer that you're my first case. I believe you should see some old guy who has had 30 or 40 cases."

"Like who?"

"Wolf at U of M and McCaffrey at the Mayo Clinic."

I visited both of them within two weeks.

Dr. Wolf, chair of Otolaryngology–Head and Neck Surgery at the University of Michigan Hospital, assured me that Dr. Richardson had done the right thing. He then brought in a Dr. Huzuka, who explained that I could become the 13th subject in the first test group for three-dimensional radiation treatment. I turned to Norene and said, "A little radiation doesn't sound too bad."

Dr. Wolf elbowed me in the shoulder. "We're going to beat the crap out of you," he said. "You'll be here five days a week for six weeks. For the last three weeks, especially, someone will have to drive you, and you will not be able to work."

I said, "I was told I should also talk to the Mayo Clinic."

"You probably should," he said. "But they're going to tell you to do the extra surgery." His forecast was correct.

I had always wanted to tour the Mayo Clinic, although not necessarily under these circumstances. During the tour, we were informed of the library in their "subway" (all the buildings are connected at the basement level) and how one could research any medical problem there. Before leaving the next morning, we went to the library and I told the attendant I wanted to read about adenoid cystic carcinoma (ACC). She said, "The new book you need to review is being looked at by that fellow over there. Here is the old book." The old book was entitled *Uncommon Cancers of the Head and Neck*. It devoted half a page to ACC. While waiting for the new book, I reviewed the survival rates of the various cancers and determined I had one of the "better" ones.

I finally got my hands on the new book, which had just come out that year. It had five pages, with pictures, discussing ACC. One line in the section regarding treatment stood out to me: "By combining postoperative radiation therapy with moderate locoregional surgery, marked mutilation and physiologic compromise are often avoided." The library made a copy for me, at no cost, and we returned home.

I gave copies of the chapter to my doctors. Dr. Richardson said, "Ron, if I were sitting in your chair, I'm not sure what I would do."

So now I was faced with a conundrum: follow the advice of the highly rated Mayo Clinic or agree to become a specimen in a test case. Fortunately, Lou Anna Simon, now provost, said, "Our medical schools are developing a cancer center and will provide whatever advice they can." I was advised to talk with Dr. Nikolay Dimitrov.

In a telephone conversation, Dr. Dimitrov said, with a heavy Russian accent, "I'll tell you what I would do. I'd talk to Dr. Shah at Sloan Kettering. I've worked with that man and I'd do whatever he advises." I was told I could possibly avoid traveling to Sloan Kettering in New York—for what would be a third or fourth opinion—by having Dr. Richardson call Dr. Shah to discuss my case. He did, and on October 8, Dr. Richardson called to inform me of Dr. Shah's opinion: "Any stray cancer cells are best eliminated by radiation."

I immediately called the University of Michigan Hospital and signed up for the three-dimensional radiation treatment. It included weekly visits to the Dental Clinic to check saliva flow from the salivary gland, which diminished each week; at the end of radiation, the large parotid gland on the right side of my jaw was essentially dead. Also, taste buds quickly were affected; within a few days, many foods became repulsive to me. By the end of radiation, a bowl of milk and crackers was delightful. (It was very moist, and I couldn't taste much of anything anyway.) However, taste buds recover rather quickly. Dry mouth did develop as forecasted, but a cup of water on the desk and one by the bed at night solved that problem.

Despite Dr. Wolf's predictions, I was able to work every day, and I drove myself to Ann Arbor and back every day, suffering very little fatigue.

This experience confirmed how fortunate we are in mid-Michigan to have great local physicians and an internationally known research hospital only 60 miles away. It's also noteworthy that the new and vastly improved radiation procedure was developed at a major research university—not an institute or clinic—reminding me of the development of Cisplatin and Carboplatin here at MSU. Barney Rosenberg, a physicist, and his team of researchers were exploring whether an electric field has an effect upon a cell's growth. This research led, serendipitously, to the development of the two compounds that have saved the lives of at least a million cancer patients, including cyclist Lance Armstrong and ice skater Scott Hamilton. I know three people personally whose lives were also saved. I never had the good fortune to meet Barney Rosenberg, even though he lived just around the corner from us on College Road.

Over the years, I've used the stories of my diagnosis and treatment to help my teammates appreciate being part of an organization that "advances knowledge and transform lives" rather than one that makes widgets or pursues some other, less noble activity. After all, our division plans, builds, and maintains the physical environment that helps facilitate the "magic."
My medical odyssey ended much better than my brother's, as Bob was diagnosed with a kidney tumor during the summer of 1993 and, regrettably, died in March of 1994 at age 57.

■ ■ ■

Joe Kavanagh elected to retire February 10, 1993, after serving MSU for more than 37 years. Joe was the first person I met in Michigan as he showed me the trailer that I eventually bought, which was next door to his. As mentioned earlier, he orchestrated my being hired as a student engineer in 1957.

The Agricultural & Livestock Education Pavilion completed in 1996, allowed the removal of the old pavilion, which was located south of the current International Center.

During the planning of the expansive campus growth during the 1960s, Joe convinced MSU to install a new 13,200V campus electrical distribution system with parallel cables, which provides enhanced reliability. He was our project representative on the Power Plant '65 construction project, stayed on as plant manager, and later became director of Power and Water.

In 1989, he agreed to transfer to the Physical Plant and become director of Maintenance and Utility Distribution. This allowed Bob Ellerhorst to become acting director of Power and Water with Joe being nearby.

Joe was keenly aware of the culture issue in our trade shops. With Don Coon's help, he identified John Buffington as the ideal leader for the shops. John proved instrumental in redeveloping a team spirit throughout the shops and with other units within the division and across campus.

Joe and his wife, Ann, continue to be close friends with Norene and me.

■ ■ ■

In early 1995, John Buffington, manager of Maintenance Services, was awarded an Excellent Progress in Achieving Diversity Award for successfully moving women into skilled trades positions. This type of recognition always embarrassed him. In this case, he pointed out that a great deal of the credit belonged to two other supervisors, Bill Behnke and Gus Gosselin. I'm convinced that their fine effort causes MSU to have, on a percentage basis, more women in skilled trades than any other organization in the United States.

During the first half of the '90s, several major projects were completed, including a major addition to the Veterinary Medical Center and the Eli Broad addition to the Business College complex. The stadium playing field was lowered six feet (to improve the sight lines for about 8,000 seats), and Beaumont Tower received a major renovation, becoming fully functional again. In addition, the "Revitalization of Michigan Agriculture" was underway, renovating Anthony Hall's Dairy Plant, replacing the Meats Lab, and building a new Livestock Education Center, a new Swine Facility, and a new Infectious Disease Containment Facility. Enhancements were made at the Dairy, Equine, Beef Cattle, and Poultry Research Centers.

There was still much more to do.

As we entered the late 1990s, one of our goals was to get the upper administration, including our new president, to recognize the need to address the deferred-maintenance backlog.

12.

Privatize?

n June 1996, I attended a Saturday morning meeting with President McPherson. Roger Wilkinson, Director of Planning and Budgets Dave Byelich, and Director of Campus Park and Planning Jeff Kacos were also present. Our goal was to give the president a better understanding of the various offices that play a role in the facilities arena.

As we were leaving the building, Peter said, "Flinn, one of these days you should give me a campus tour."

"How about now?"

He agreed. I asked Jeff Kacos to join us.

The three of us jumped into my car. As we were rounding Circle Drive, I said, "Here's another building that needs to be removed," pointing to Morrill Hall.

"You're probably right," Peter said, "but I'm trying to get around the emotional fact that my mother spent four years in that corner room while attending MSC."

Morrill Hall had been built in 1900 as a women's dormitory and gymnasium. Unfortunately, the structural system was entirely timber, and the long span of the floor joists allowed the floors to flex, cracking all floor finishes

span of the floor joists allowed the floors to flex, cracking all floor finishes such as tiles and linoleum. All of the other building systems, exterior walls, windows, and heating and electrical systems were antiquated and at the end of their life. In attempting to gain support for removal rather than rebuilding, I began referring to the building as "a cesspool for dollars." (One approach in addressing deferred maintenance is to remove any and all facilities that have an unjustifiable repair cost.)

Later that year, Jeff Kacos and I were asked to present a report on the status and development of the campus facilities to the Board of Trustees. University Engineer Bob Nestle and Assistant Director of Facilities Planning and Space Management Bill Latta joined us on the panel. The core subject was a 40-year history of the East Lansing campus and the facilities organizations, which was well received. But as I started to describe the condition and age of major systems in certain buildings, as a precursor to presenting the deferred-maintenance challenge, the audience lost interest. There was no point in continuing, so I ended the presentation. This reinforced my conviction that getting MSU to acknowledge the existence of a major deferred-maintenance problem—and agree to develop a financial solution—might become the biggest challenge of my career.

■ ■ ■

Peter McPherson was exploring different ideas about how to solve MSU's "structural deficit"—the school has always had inadequate funds to address its mission—and one day said, "Maybe we should sell the power plant." (When I heard him say that, I thought, *I may need to outlive this guy!*) Some time later, Steve Yambor, with Black and Veatch, identified an individual who made his living buying and operating power plants and was willing to visit and review our plant.

At the end of the man's visit, he said, "I've never seen a power plant this large being operated by so few people. I can't afford to buy your plant unless I'm allowed to significantly raise the rates and obtain a decent ROI [Return on Investment]."

A number of months later, a trustee asked if the selling idea was still valid. Peter told him, "Selling the power plant is similar to borrowing money. As a university, we can borrow money cheaper than anyone else, but we cannot afford to have our utility costs increase."

"Privatization" was a popular subject during the '90s, and it is a topic that has always intrigued me. There's no question that large construction projects and other intermittent assignments are best performed by private firms. My years of experience as an in-house service provider, as well as listening to many tales of attempted privatization at other institutions, have convinced me that a university is best served by a dedicated, productive in-house staff to perform the repeated activities of maintenance and operations. However, if an organization has become unproductive, too expensive, and unwilling to change, I would recommend privatization. I elaborated on this subject in my article "Privatization in Today's Facilities Operation," published in the January 1996 issue of APPA's *Facility Manager* magazine.

While I was the international president of APPA during 1996–97, I got to spend quite a bit of time with Wayne Leroy, who had replaced Walt Shaw as APPA's executive vice president. Wayne told me about attending a meeting of several university presidents who were discussing privatization. They all agreed that one starts out thinking, *Maybe we can save some money if we privatize some of our facility responsibilities.* At the end of the meeting, they all agreed that the decision of whether or not to privatize is really based on two questions: "Is the unit responsive?" (One president reported he had to telephone his Grounds department three times to get the grass mowed for commencement!) and "Does the leadership of the organization 'keep the saw sharp' for the troops?" (In other words, is the staff receiving the training and equipment to be efficient and motivated?)

■   ■   ■

As APPA president, one is expected to visit as many regional meetings as possible, but I was surprised to learn it was also a tradition to attend the Georgia state meeting, GAPPA, which is held each Memorial Day weekend on Jekyll Island.

During the weekend, our host asked me to officially install the incoming officers at that evening's banquet. I agreed but thought, *Wow, I didn't prepare for this.* Fortunately, I had a couple of hours to think about how to handle this request. I recalled the NSPE installation format that I used as vice president of MSPE, when I installed officers at a number of local chapters, albeit many years earlier. From memory, I reviewed the basics. I would have the incoming officers stand before the audience and pledge "to faithfully discharge the duties," etc. The additional wrinkle I added was to then ask all the members of the organization in the audience to stand and pledge to assist the new officers "whenever called upon." Wayne asked for a copy of my notes from that ceremony, and I understand this now has become the format for all APPA officer installations.

As I was finishing my year as APPA president, Tom Vacha, from the University of Delaware and APPA's president elect, died two days before the installation ceremony. The APPA Board was stunned and asked, "What do we do now?" I answered, "We need to follow the steps taken in 1971 when President Elect Bob Houston died. But we need to move swiftly as we only have two days. All of the unsuccessful candidates from past elections should be serious contenders." Several were contacted, and two agreed to present themselves to the Board. Pieter van der Have from the University of Utah was selected.

Shortly after I became past president, I was informed that Wayne Leroy had decided not to renew his contract as executive vice president. Some of the Board members were convinced that a nationwide search for a new association executive should take place.

I called Pieter. I said, "I don't want to go behind your back, since you're the president, but I believe Lander Medlin, assistant executive vice president, should be promoted to the executive VP position." He agreed and was pleased that I was going to call all the Board members necessary to obtain a unanimous vote. In my telephone conversations with the Board members, I pointed out how well Ms. Medlin had served me while I was president. I also related how I first met Lander in 1984 when she came to MSU as a member of a Physical Plant team from the University of Maryland to review how we processed work orders. "She's one of us," I explained.

Lander became the executive vice president and continues in that role today. I'm convinced that if she's not the best association executive in the country, she's in the top five.

■   ■   ■

Early in the 1990s, I met with a small committee to determine how MSU should acquire a law school. (In the mid-1960s, John Hannah had said that a good university needs a law school, but the Michigan Legislature told him, "Don't look to us for funding." Over the years, I'd wondered if Hannah's vision would ever be achieved.)

The Detroit College of Law at MSU (now the MSU College of Law) built in 1997.

President McPherson told the committee that he had been contacted to see if there was any interest in the Detroit College of Law (DCL) becoming part of MSU. One of the committee members had a copy of a year-old *Detroit Free Press* newspaper, which had an article stating DCL was going to Oakland University.

Peter turned to me and said, "You need to find out what kind of facilities Oakland University is planning to provide for them, without anyone knowing what you're doing." This was my first "covert-operations request" from Peter. (I learned that Oakland University was proposing to locate the Law library on the top floor of the university's main library. Law schools much prefer to have their library located within their law building.)

We reviewed several facilities in the Detroit area to determine if they could become a new home for the law college. (Some of the buildings we looked at had armed guards.) Again, we could tell no one what we were doing.

Finally, we decided that the best answer was to build a new building on the East Lansing campus. Peter was in China when he was informed of our estimated cost for the structure. I'm told he was unhappy with the figure and said, "Gee, do I have to go back and fire those guys?" His response echoed one of his favorite phrases: "I'm cheap, damn it, and I'm proud of it." After the law school was built, Peter made it known that he felt the building was more "ritzy" than necessary. However, former President Cecil Mackey told him, "If this Law building doesn't look like the newest and nicest, we may have difficulty in acquiring accreditation."

■ ■ ■

Although one could tire of Peter continually challenging the cost of construction and alterations—we had numerous meetings about that—there's no disputing his agility in the political arena.

For example, in the mid-1990s, we were in need of significantly more research space, but the State wanted to fund only additions or renovations. In a campus meeting, Peter asked a group of us, "Are you telling me I need to go downtown and convince Governor Engler we need a new building?" We said yes. As a result of his efforts, we were funded for the Biomedical and Physical Sciences building.

His political connections extended far beyond the state's borders, though. He frequently hosted prominent political leaders on campus, including President Bill Clinton and National Security Advisor Condoleezza Rice.

He was also effective in media relations. While John DiBiaggio was negatively written up for installing a larger awning over the backyard deck of Cowles House, Peter enclosed the deck, thereby expanding the house for all seasons, without a mention in the newspapers.

I will particularly remember him for mounting a campaign to significantly increase the number of trees south of the river. He thought that, in time, the south campus should resemble the north campus as much as possible. As someone who appreciates the impact and importance of trees, I thought that was a good idea.

■ ■ ■

In January 1998, Mark Murray, former director of the Michigan Department of Management and Budget, became associate vice president for Business and Finance at MSU. On September 1, he became vice president, as Roger Wilkinson retired after serving MSU for 39 years.

Shortly after Mark arrived, Roger Wilkinson turned over to him a written proposal from CATA (Capital Area Transportation Authority) to merge the MSU bus system into their organization. (There had been discussions and meetings about this, on and off, for more than two decades. But CATA didn't appear to get serious until the mid-1990s.)

Mark had the added perspective of having actually driven a CATA bus while attending MSU. He enlisted Gene Garrison, manager of Automotive Services, and Mike Rice, with the MSU Department of Public Safety, to assist him in negotiating with CATA.

In October 1998, Mark decided to reorganize the solid waste operations and assign them to the Physical Plant. I was to receive Recycling Services and Waste Removal (the garbage trucks). I pointed out that by not including the Surplus Store as well, he was giving me only limited authority in recycling and disposing of stuff; the Surplus Store recycles discarded items back into the campus, sells items it cannot recycle, or, worst case, sends them to the landfill. I further pointed out that any partially loaded garbage truck needs to be parked in a heated space during freezing weather, and the Grounds Department no longer wanted them in their building. (If a load of garbage becomes frozen in a truck, it will not dump.) Mark said he was sure I could make it work.

In other institutions, the solid waste operation typically would be assigned to Custodial. I surprised many individuals when I asked Bob Ellerhorst, with Power and Water, to take it on. My decision was based on the fact that Bob had once chosen to send fly ash, the residue from pulverized coal boilers, to a cement factory rather than to the landfill. His decision resulted in a $400,000 annual cost avoidance in tipping fees. This was the best recycling/solid waste disposal achievement ever experienced on our campus.

During 1998, we began planning an Executive Development Center for the College of Business, to be located next to the University Club. Mark called and asked, "Ron, what's wrong with designing and building a building as low cost as possible, knowing it will survive only 30 years, if the function it's being built for ends after 30 years?"

I'm sure the answer he wanted from me was, "Nothing." But I replied, "We tend not to tear down buildings if they can be repurposed for another function, as we're always short of space."

He said, "We're convinced we can do it," and hung up. I interpreted the "We" as he and Peter. They were convinced there was a way to build a building cheaper than having the Physical Plant handle the project. They decided to use the design-build approach—rather than the design-bid-build approach—which can save money and time but can sometimes lead to situations where contractors make project decisions they are not qualified to make.

In late December, Mark Murray abruptly left and returned to the State of Michigan as its treasurer.

On January 10, 1999, the Board of Trustees appointed Fred Poston as treasurer and interim vice president of Business and Finance. Fred and I had become well acquainted when he was dean of Agriculture and we worked together on the "Revitalization of Michigan Agriculture" project.

Gerry Haarer, director of Land Management, was no fan of the Physical Plant. He saw no need for engineers, as he had built many pole barns for Mahogany Farms before he joined MSU. I was sure he, along with other critics of the Physical Plant, had told many a tale to the new VP. This was confirmed one day in a meeting when Fred stopped in midsentence, turned to me, and asked, "How can you enjoy your job?"

"A thick hide helps," I told him.

That he would even ask the question—implying he was well aware of the criticisms—was further proof that the Physical Plant still had a challenge in customer relations. My immediate goal was to convince Fred that our "too slow, too expensive" image was more myth than fact.

While Fred was still dean, and as we were approaching the completion of the "Revitalization of Michigan Agriculture," he asked for a meeting.

"I remember," he began, "as we were underway with this project, asking you what happens to any dollars left in the contingency fund when the project was finished. You said they would be mine. Now I'm being told there are no funds left."

"You're correct on both accounts."

He became agitated. "I was planning on building a laboratory that was left out of the plans, along with a library in the attic space of Anthony Hall that you and I helped clean out some years ago."

I thought, *This would be a good time to display some flexibility on our part.*

"Well," I said, "as you know, we're not budgeted to fund alterations. But we'll make the laboratory happen. I'll also commit my team to build your library and thereby keep the cost as low as possible."

"Good. I'm sure I can raise the funds for the library."

The Radiology Building completed in 1998 and funded by income earned by the Radiology Department. Jim Potchen returned to MSU in 1975, committed to developing a Radiology Department, and was allotted space in the basement of Olin Health Center. The current cutting-edge facility is a testament to his outstanding entrepreneurial leadership.

My agreeing to help the college by bending certain rules caused Fred to know the Physical Plant wasn't totally "inflexible and uncaring." It also helped me make a positive impression on the man who, in just a few years, would end up becoming my boss!

Fred had barely moved into the VP's office when I sent him an e-mail regarding CATA taking over the MSU bus system. I had two concerns. First, I thought MSU should have representation on the CATA Board. Second, I believed that any of our bus drivers who chose to transfer to CATA should retain their seniority. After a brief discussion, Fred agreed. At the April 1999 Board of Trustees meeting, the MSU administration was authorized to sell 14 buses to CATA and to allow CATA to take over the campus bus routes.

Many folks were convinced I was unhappy with CATA assuming the campus busing routes. Actually, I was agreeable if the cost to MSU was reasonable. The MSU bus system had never received any financial support from the university, covering its costs with funds coming from the fare box and ticket sales. As a result, we never seemed to have enough buses during inclement weather to satisfy the demand.

After the transfer was finished, I was surprised to be asked numerous times, "How do you feel about being privatized?"

"You seem to be confused," I'd tell them. "*We* were the Private entity with no subsidies; CATA is a *Public* entity, supported by both Federal and State government as well as a local millage."

■   ■   ■

In June 1999, bids were received for the proposed Biomedical and Physical Sciences building. They exceeded the budget by $5,400,000. Fred was pleased and impressed when Bob Nestle, working with the SHG design team and the Christman Construction Company, value engineered the project back within budget in less than three weeks.

Fred was the first VP to take a keen interest in the color of bricks used on new buildings and additions. He initially thought the bricks on the Ag Hall addition were a poor match. I suggested we wait until they were washed down. (After completion, a new brick wall requires an acid washing to remove any mortar scum and reveal its true color.) After some time, he became comfortable with the recommendations of the brick committee, who are zealots at obtaining good brick matches for the campus buildings.

Fred would frequently joke, "They never included *that* topic when I was in entomology class" when discussing a facility issue. But despite his feigned ignorance, he was genuinely interested in and committed to enhancing campus construction. One day he said, "Flinn, what are you going to do about those 'energy hog' buildings like Ag Hall?"

I told him, "Fred, Ag Hall is a *good* one."

"But you showed me how the 90-year-old windows bow out and allow cold air to enter."

"That's also the only fresh air the building receives, and the steam radiators under the windows provide the required warming. Real 'energy hog' buildings are the Chemistry building and others with fume hoods in research labs, which require 100 percent fresh air that is then totally exhausted."

I was pleased to have a VP who was truly interested in the details of the campus facilities.

■   ■   ■

Besides the Detroit College of Law building and the addition to Ag Hall, we constructed the Food Safety and Toxicology building, the Radiology building, and an addition to the Duffy Daugherty building (providing academic study space for student athletes) during the late 1990s.

As we approached the new century, there was growing apprehension that many of our campus computers would not be able to handle the date shift from 1999 to 2000, potentially leading to data loss and system outages.

New Century

The widespread fear that many computers would be unable to handle the date changing from 1999 to 2000, known as "Y2K," caused me to plan on being home at midnight on December 31, 1999. However, our good friends Bob and Sue Oaks pushed Norene and me hard to spend New Year's Eve with them in their new home in Ann Arbor. Bob Ellerhorst was going to be at the power plant overnight, so I asked him to call me at 12:01 A.M. and confirm that everything was up and running.

It turned out that most of the worldwide Y2K panic was for nothing. When Bob called to tell me everything was fine at the power plant, he paused, then said, "Have you heard about the Ag Hall fire?"

"No," I said. "How big is it?"

"I was told it is about the size of the laboratory fire in the Chemistry building a few months ago."

I hung up thinking, *Any fire is bad news, but it doesn't sound too serious.*

The next morning, when Norene and I got back home, the answering machine was filled with calls reporting a major catastrophe. What a way to start the new year!

I immediately drove to Ag Hall.

It was obvious this had been a major fire, burning the upper floors and roof at the northeast corner of the building. Fortunately, a building occupant—thank goodness he was spending New Year's Eve there—smelled smoke and called the fire department. Otherwise, we would have lost the whole building. Numerous Physical Plant staff members also were on campus, to ensure the Y2K transition was problem free, and quickly responded to the emergency. The first cleanup group to respond were MSU custodians who, on Saturday, January 1, gave up their holiday and the opportunity to watch the MSU Spartans win the Florida Citrus Bowl.

In extinguishing the fire, the East Lansing Fire Department had to pour huge quantities of water onto the roof, which, due to roof damage, ended up flowing down into the building, flooding all the lower floors. The Physical Plant roofing crew installed a temporary roof as soon as they were allowed to take action. However, investigative teams from MSU police, the Bureau of Alcohol, Tobacco, and Firearms (ATF), and the FBI were on site to collect and secure all evidence before turning the building over to our team. The Earth Liberation Front (ELF) claimed responsibility for starting the fire, protesting agricultural biotechnology/genetic engineering. After the initial cleanup and installation of temporary weather barriers, we hired a contractor who specializes in fire repairs to repair all damage and eliminate any possibility of mold developing. The final cost exceeded $1 million.

The Ag Hall fire was MSU's second brush with on-campus terrorism. Back in 1992, an animal-rights group fire bombed a research suite in Anthony Hall, destroying over 30 years of research.

However, the September 11, 2001, attacks in New York City and Washington, DC, exemplified terrorism on an international scale. They led us to take a much closer look at potential vulnerabilities within MSU's facilities. One of our first steps was to erect a barrier wall in front of a bank of transformers at the power plant.

■ ■ ■

As vice president, Fred Poston was getting acquainted with the facilities side of the campus. He was more than amazed at some of his findings. For example, the Physical Plant did not have detailed records on who had possession of the 30,000 keys that had been issued. Further, a person could receive their final paycheck without showing a slip from the key shop confirming that they had returned all MSU keys issued to them. (MSU's policy called for the colleges and academic departments to distribute the keys and keep their own records.) All the universities he had served previously had tight controls regarding building keys. He decided to promote the installation of swipe-card systems on new buildings and to develop a long-range plan for making the campus keyless.

Fred had become familiar with construction issues as we planned and built the "Revitalization of Michigan Agriculture" projects. Now he was the one to present all proposed construction projects to the Board of Trustees. Therefore, he and I were in frequent discussions. He was particularly curious about the design-build approach being taken with the new Executive Development Center (now known as the Henry Center). By the time the project was completed, though, he was convinced not to use design-build on future projects; there was no cost savings, there were a few questionable design features, and the roof leaked.

This is a good time to review a couple of comments we frequently hear regarding the quality and cost of university buildings. (I've never seen a campus construction project that wasn't viewed as "too expensive," regardless of cost.)

"It's unrealistic to construct a building to last 100 years." Where I came from in central New York, a 100-year-old house is no big deal. Any house that is properly built and maintained will last 100 years. And that doesn't only apply to houses. Ag Hall, built properly in 1909, is ready to serve another 100 years. (Admittedly, a modern HVAC renovation would provide added comfort for the occupants.) Long-life facilities are important to enduring universities, but many people don't consider the probable life of a university when making construction decisions.

"Why does it cost so much to build on a university campus?" Over the years, the MSU Physical Plant developed a number of responses to this question. But the best response I've seen was developed by two of my Big 10 colleagues, Donald J. Guckert and Jeri Ripley King at the University of Iowa. Don and Jeri show what additional features "Your House on Campus" would need to satisfy all the codes and requirements that must be incorporated when constructing a campus building, all of which significantly increase the cost. (They describe this in "The High Cost of Building a Better University," published in APPA's May/June 2003 *Facilities Manager* magazine.)

. . .

One day Fred asked, "Does MSU have a Master Plan?" I told him we hadn't really had a Master Plan since John Hannah left. He wanted to change that.

The new Campus Master Plan Work Team worked with Sasaki Associates from Massachusetts to produce the Campus Master Plan Executive Summary on December 7, 2001. It is commonly called the 2020 Plan. Among its conclusions was confirmation that many building additions could occur without densification of the campus. Therefore, there was little need to continue campus sprawl.

. . .

Having the responsibility for recycling, Bob Ellerhorst recommended that we gain access to a facility that could house a baler; white paper and cardboard, when baled, garner a higher price. Fred thought we should determine if other local entities would be willing to join us in solving what he viewed as a regional recycling challenge, not merely an MSU issue. During a meeting at Kellogg Center, Fred made it clear that if MSU were going at it alone, we were not going to provide services for other entities. Only the City of Lansing indicated interest in pursuing a joint solution.

Lansing already had a recycling building, and their team was agreeable to the idea of installing a sorting line and baler. MSU had funds available from previous sales of recyclables to buy the necessary equipment. However, the shape of the building wasn't ideal, and we needed an expert opinion as to whether it would work. Ideally, we wanted quotes from experienced installation contractors and suppliers. We prepared a Request for Proposals and distributed it to all interested parties. Two weeks before the scheduled date to receive proposals, we were told that, for legal reasons, they could not be opened within the Lansing city limits, so we changed the location to the MSU Purchasing Office.

A number of days later, the Lansing recycling team was summoned to a meeting with some of the city council, chaired by Councilwoman Carol Wood. They were relieved when Bob Ellerhorst and I agreed to join them.

At the meeting, Councilwoman Wood was severely tongue lashing the Lansing recyclers for daring to take bids on altering a Lansing facility without first receiving council approval. I raised my hand and explained I was the guilty party and was unaware of the Lansing policy. I further explained that what we did was "standard operating procedure" on the MSU campus. She expressed additional displeasure and then dismissed us. As we walked out, I passed Trustee Ferguson, who was there for other business. He said, "We trustees have never treated you this badly, have we?" I certainly agreed. After David Hollister left the mayor's office, any interest in an MSU–Lansing merger soon waned.

We proposed building an MSU recycling facility, but the president wasn't supportive, even if we could provide a five-year payback. The idea was shelved.

■   ■   ■

Fred and I continued to have conversations regarding sustainability. He was pleased that we had sampled hybrid automobiles as soon as they had become available, and he urged us to increase the number in our fleet. He was equally pleased with the various steps we had taken to assure the campus was using energy prudently.

During one of our conversations, I said, "We have all these buildings, all this acreage, a large population, large herds of animals, and we have our arms around everything that comes in and goes out of the campus. We should be creating sustainability models for other communities in Michigan and across the country." I could see I'd struck a responsive chord. We started developing ways to implement the idea.

■   ■   ■

Upon learning the facts regarding our deferred-maintenance situation, Fred attempted to obtain support from the trustees and other key administrators and, in the process, came up with a presentation and new catch phrase. He would point out that the MSU Physical Plant squeezes more years of service out of the building and utility systems than any other organization he ever heard of, but the trick is to replace things "just in time" before they fail. This was masterful, as the words "deferred maintenance" have very little punch.

Support from the president was meager until May 29, 2002, when I presented Fred with the photographs of the cooling-tower failure at the Regional Chilled Water Plant. The large fan blades on Cooling Tower No. 1, installed in 1971, flew apart, sending one blade flying across a sidewalk and landing in the street. Fred immediately took the pictures to Peter McPherson, who exclaimed, "Geez, that could be dangerous!"

"Flinn's been telling us this stuff doesn't last forever," Fred replied.

This opened the door for Fred to deliver a formal presentation regarding maintenance needs to the Board of Trustees at their summer retreat at Crystal Mountain, Michigan, on August 8, 2002.

■   ■   ■

As we entered the new century, we were well aware that the campus peak electrical demand would exceed our firm electrical capacity by 2002. To avoid rolling blackouts, our firm capacity needed to be enlarged.

Increasing the capacity of the Consumers Energy (CE) substation appeared to be the most economical approach. The substation's capacity was 21MW, and we proposed to increase it to 40MW. Unfortunately, the 46kV transmission line feeding the substation could not handle 40MW, so a new 138kV tie-line was required. Complicating the effort was the deregulation of the electrical industry, which caused CE to spin off electrical transmission to a new entity, Michigan Electrical Transmission Company (METC). By August 2003, though, we finally received a contract for signature.

On August 14, an East Coast blackout occurred that spread into the Midwest, including CE's system. The Simon plant's electrical relay switches separated us from the affected grid, and the main campus continued to be powered up by the Simon plant's generators. However, the farm district, including our major campus wells, lost power; within a couple of hours we were confronted with a water supply crisis. The CE power came back on just as we were about to take emergency steps. Nevertheless, the situation was very disconcerting. A few years earlier, after a similar lengthy outage in the farm district, CE pledged that MSU would *never* experience another such outage.

I called Fred and said, "We need to change our plans. If we had been purchasing a large amount of electricity through the substation when the blackout occurred, the whole campus would have gone black!" He agreed.

At the December 2003 Board of Trustees meeting, I was asked to present the proposed solution. I recommended adding a 24MW steam-driven electrical generator and a 14MW natural gas combustion turbine electrical generator with a heat recovery boiler on the combustion turbine's exhaust. The combustion turbine provides "black start" functionality, capable of

The Stadium Tower finished in 2006.

restarting the power plant if the tie-line faults and blackens the plant. The trustees approved proceeding at an estimated cost of $84.3 million.

We also purchased six very large, trailer-mounted, diesel-driven electrical generators. Each one is more than capable of powering up a campus well, ensuring water will always be available to the university.

■   ■   ■

During this same time period, the Athletic department was investigating various solutions to the dated Press Deck and President Box at Spartan Stadium. Other universities had built some elaborate towers that included suites. A quick tour of two or three convinced Fred that such an expansion looked feasible for MSU as well, but first we had to get the president on board.

We met with Peter McPherson and HNTB Consultants, who brought a conceptual drawing and renderings. Peter barely sat down before he asked, "How much?" When told it would be in the range of $60 million, he got up and started to walk out. Greg Ianni, associate director of Athletic Facilities, stopped him. "Don't you even want to hear the game plan for paying for it?" he asked. This caused Peter to agree to spend a few more minutes at the meeting. Ianni was able to show that the project wasn't beyond the department's ability to fund it. Peter approved moving on to the next step in planning.

Greg Ianni, an alumnus, had returned to MSU in 1993 after serving in a similar role in the Athletic department of Ohio University. From my viewpoint, this was one of the best things to happen in the Athletic department. Greg is a true team player and uses "what's best for MSU" as a credo. The improvement to athletic facilities since his arrival is astounding and helps explain why he's now the deputy athletics director.

■   ■   ■

During the first half of the new decade, we replaced the Shaw Lane parking ramp, built the Diagnostic Center for Population and Animal Health, expanded the International Center with the Delia Koo Addition, constructed a composting facility at the Dairy Research Center, and completed many other smaller projects. Also, the Michigan Department of Transportation extended Trowbridge Road into the campus, which is now the primary entrance for visitors coming off the interstate highway.

The Physical Plant's organization also changed. Gene Garrison retired, and I elected to transfer Transportation Services to Roy Simon, as his Telecommunication Services also receives no General Fund dollars; both units are financially self-supporting. I finally capitulated to Gus Gosselin's request for an in-house safety officer and asked Mel Latnie to leave Custodial and become the division's Safety and Climate officer. I then asked Gus to head up the newly recreated Building Service department, combining Custodial with Maintenance once again.

In late 2004, Fred Poston announced the transfer of the Grounds department to the Physical Plant division, effective January 1, 2005 (70 years since its separation in 1944). Additionally, the landscape architects were joining the design team in Engineering and Architectural Services.

Peter McPherson announced he would leave MSU on January 1, 2005.

We now looked forward to a new era with a new president.

14.

New Era

Our new president, Lou Anna Simon, was no stranger to MSU. She had arrived here in 1970 to earn a PhD in Administration and Higher Education. After earning her doctorate in 1974, she became a faculty member and assistant director of the Office of Institutional Research (now Planning and Budgets). Over the decades, she moved up through the ranks—assistant provost, associate provost, and provost. As early as 1985, Roger Wilkinson had said, "No one knows this university better than Lou Anna."

■   ■   ■

With the Grounds department now part of the Physical Plant, I met with all the full-time employees and became familiar with their organization structure and approach to job assignments.

During this time, Gary Parrott, Grounds manager, informed me that he was seriously considering retirement. Fortunately, I was able to persuade him to stay another year before I needed to search for a new manager.

Sherrie Lovich, manager of Business and Personnel, became a mother and decided to leave the work world. She suggested I consider Barb Wilber as her replacement. Barb had started working here as a student employee, as had Sherrie, but Barb worked in the Central Control office, moved to construction inspection (Law building), and then moved back to Maintenance as the supervisor of customer projects. With this wide range of experience, she certainly knew our organization. And then, unsolicited, Ken Crowell, manager of Skilled Trades, also suggested Barb to me. I've learned that when you receive recommendations from people you highly regard, you should seriously consider their advice. So Barb replaced Sherrie, and she continues to do a great job in managing the Business office (now known as Support Services).

During a 2006 meeting with Fred Poston, Bob Ellerhorst and I got a clear message that he thought the university needed an energy and environmental engineer, a person to spend full time focusing on energy conservation and utilization of existing buildings and proposed buildings. Bob and I went to lunch. As I was ticking off the attributes one should have for such an assignment, he exclaimed, "That's Lynda Boomer!" I had to agree. She had even become LEED (Leadership in Energy and Environmental Design) certified before most of us knew what that meant. The Engineering office was not thrilled that I was asking Lynda to report directly to me. Dan Bollman said, "You're taking my best project person!" My retort was, "You wouldn't expect me to take anyone but the best, would you?"

■   ■   ■

Gus Gosselin and Tim Potter, both avid cyclists, had numerous conversations with Fred Poston about establishing a bicycle shop on campus. Fred had advocated from early on that any road rebuilding should also include bike lanes, making the campus more bicycle-friendly.

One day Gus said to me, "Fred wonders if you would be agreeable to having a bicycle unit as part of the Physical Plant?" I told him I thought it could work as part of Transportation Services. In fall 2006, we launched MSU Bikes, with Tim Potter as manager.

■   ■   ■

In 2007, approval was granted to begin schematic design for a new medical building—the College of Human Medicine—in Grand Rapids.

The Residential College for Arts and Letters was completed by squeezing a large new building in between Snyder and Phillips Halls. The project included

The Eli and Edythe Broad Art Museum completed in 2012.

a stunning new-style food-service facility, the Gallery, which continues to be a favorite lunch spot for students and faculty.

The original University Village Apartments, built in the early 1950s, were demolished and replaced with modern air-conditioned apartments.

Following Gary Parrott's retirement, Gerry Dobbs became manager of Grounds after a nationwide search. Gerry came from an arboretum in Kentucky and had prior experience working with universities and municipalities. Within a few months, an employee committee recommended the department title be changed to Landscape Services, which is more indicative of the unit's broad responsibilities. With significant support from Site Improvement and Nursery Supervisor Adam Lawver, the Beaumont Nursery, which grows replacement trees for the campus, expanded into providing site-improvement materials (including topsoil) and recycling broken concrete and asphalt. The expanded activities have made the nursery a profit center.

Mel Latnie retired and Andy Smith became the safety officer. With Fred Poston's urging, I agreed Andy would jointly report to me and Kevin

Eisenbeis, director of Environmental Health and Safety (EHS). Andy came from EHS and continues to attend their weekly meeting, staying up to date on the latest regulations.

In 2008, we added on to the Chemistry building, which cleverly pushed the upper floors toward eastbound Shaw Lane while maintaining a decent setback at the first-floor level.

The Skandalaris Addition to the Duffy Daugherty building provided a grand entry foyer for this ever-expanding facility.

■ ■ ■

In October 2008, we were asked to place a large banner on Circle IM reading, "BRING THE FRIB TO OUR CRIB." ("FRIB" is shorthand for "Facility for Rare Isotope Beams.") Presidential candidate Barack Obama was making a campaign stop at MSU's Adams Field, and he would be able to see the banner while speaking on the podium.

Our campaign to win the FRIB project was a lengthy one. Several years earlier, in a conversation with Konrad Gelbke, director of the Cyclotron Laboratory, I asked, "What do you think our chances are in winning versus Argonne Laboratories in Illinois?" Conrad replied, "You need to realize that all such facilities exist at various laboratories across the United States. They aren't at universities. During a committee meeting in Washington, DC, I suggested we consider a university campus. I thought I might be laughed out of the room, but another attendee supported the idea. Even so, the contest we're facing is like an ice-skating competition between the USA and Russia. MSU is the USA, while every other facility is Russia—and all the *judges* are Russians."

There were many meetings with review panels, who were determining if MSU had the goods to deliver this project. The researchers and faculty were highly regarded, but there were questions about the support side. During the review period, construction of a long tunnel was being proposed; Bob Nestle convinced them of our expertise by showing pictures of the Bogue Street tunnel installed a few years earlier. When Bob Ellerhorst presented the depth of reliability for electrical power—99 MW in-house generation, 21MW from the grid, and black-start capability—the response was, "We've never had redundancy like that at any of our other laboratories!"

With great support from our congressional delegation, Senators Stabenow

The South Farm Lane Underpass built in 2009.

and Levin and Representative Rogers, we were successful. (It's possible that the jailing of Illinois Governor Blagojevich and the FBI's report regarding corruption in the state of Illinois also helped the decision to go our way and place this $730 million project at MSU.)

Once construction started, MSU Construction Superintendent Brad Bull transferred to the FRIB site to become the director of Conventional Facilities and Infrastructure.

■ ■ ■

In 2009, the Surplus Store and Recycling Facility was completed. This is the best recycling facility in mid-Michigan and, I believe, one of the best in the country. The open drop-off feature, available to one and all, is a big hit with the residents of the region. The surplus store continues to draw large crowds on sale days.

The Demmer Shooting Facility was also completed and provides young athletes the opportunity to train from the ground up to become the next

Olympian or Paralympian. The indoor and outdoor archery ranges, as well as the indoor firearm ranges, are also very popular with local citizens.

The Farm Lane Underpass Project was also finished, constructed as an MDOT project. Again, Senator Stabenow was a strong supporter and helped to facilitate federal funding. She recalled being delayed numerous times on campus by a stopped train blocking Farm Lane. Yet there was more at stake than mere annoyance. All too frequently, pedestrians (some with bicycles slung over their shoulders) were seen squeezing between the cars of temporarily stopped trains. It was truly a tragedy waiting to happen.

As early as 1963, I participated in studies of how to quickly get emergency vehicles to Spartan Village while a stopped train was blocking Harrison Road. We determined that raising or lowering Harrison Road was virtually impossible. A few years later, the proposed Cross Campus Highway Project included lowering Bogue Street below the highway and Canadian National railroad tracks. However, that project never materialized. Living south of the campus for decades, and frequently delayed on ether Harrison Road or Farm Lane, I thought I would never see the problem solved. In the end, it had only taken 45-plus years.

■   ■   ■

In 2009, the campus faced an across-the-board four-percent budget reduction. Fred Poston suggested the Physical Plant reduce its budget by stopping office cleaning, since our funding only allowed us to visit once a month and, at that rate, most occupants did not even notice the effort. His letter to the campus stated, "While this is not a preferred outcome, it is necessary in an attempt to balance the budget."

Some months later, the leadership in Custodial Services became aware of a work assignment program for custodians called OS1 by ManageMen. Implementation during 2010 allowed custodians to once again visit offices *once a week* without *any* budget increase. This increase in productivity has virtually made our custodians "bulletproof" when potential areas for privatization are discussed.

The year 2010 brought completion of the $90 million Secchia Center in Grand Rapids, providing classroom space for the College of Human Medicine as well as a new headquarters. The renovation of Brody Hall (aka "Ma Brody") was completed in 2011 and provided a new restaurant venue similar to what was installed in Snyder–Phillips.

We also removed a major landmark: the smoke stack at the Shaw Lane Power Plant. Many people had nostalgic feelings for the structure; the white bricks spelled out "MSC" and many used it as a beacon to find Spartan Stadium. However, the smoke stack was last used in 1974, and the ravages of weathering had greatly increased the probability of bricks falling, thus creating a dangerous situation.

In April 2012, the Board of Trustees approved proceeding with the South Campus Anaerobic Digester to be built at the Dairy Research, Teaching, and Extension Center. This facility consumes food wastes—which otherwise would go to the landfill or sewage plant—and produces electricity, which lowers electrical costs in the farm district. This facility, coupled with the nearby Manure Composting Facility, makes for a very "green" complex and greatly reduces MSU's environmental footprint.

Several major construction projects were completed in 2012. An addition to Wells Hall provided space for faculty members to move from Morrill Hall, allowing for its demolition a few months later. A Molecular Plant Science addition to the Plant and Soil Science building provided much-needed laboratory space. The Bott Nursing Education Wing was connected to the Life Sciences building and provided the college with its own home.

The first phase of replacing the steam distribution on North Campus took place during the summer, causing major disruption as both roads and sidewalks at various locations needed to be closed. Unfortunately, the 100-year-old tunnels were failing structurally and needed to be replaced. Three more phases, in subsequent years, were needed to complete the project around the North Campus Circle Drive.

The most dramatic project, however, was the Eli and Edythe Broad Art Museum. This was MSU's first signature project by a signature architect, Zaha Hadid. It appears people either love it or hate it. Whenever I encounter a detractor, I ask if they're familiar with the Sydney Opera House. They usually are. I tell them it was controversial when it was first built. Yet today, it is immediately recognizable, and Australia now uses it as its national symbol. I am convinced that the Broad Museum, over time, may play a similar role for MSU.

In October 2012, Sean O'Connor took over as manager of Landscape Services as Gerry Dobbs left to pursue other career opportunities.

■　■　■

As a member of the Michigan Farm Bureau, I was aware of discontent on the part of some factions of the agricultural community regarding their perception of MSU's support, or lack thereof. Thus, it wasn't too surprising to see Fred Poston agreeing to once again become dean of Agriculture as he had been the best of the best. He was officially appointed by the Board of Trustees at their October 26 meeting.

President Simon met with each of Fred's former direct reports to gain our opinions as to what reorganization should occur. By early December, she decided to recommend three new vice president positions to the Board of Trustees: Vennie Gore, assistant vice president for Residential and Hospitality Services, would become vice president for Auxiliary Enterprises; Mark Haas, associate vice president for Finance and chief financial officer, would become vice president for Finance and Treasurer; and my title would change from assistant vice president for Physical Plant to vice president for Strategic Infrastructure Planning and Facilities. These positions became effective January 1, 2013.

During my discussions with the president, I confided that, given my age, my retirement should be sooner rather than later. Norene had been urging me to retire for some time.

My letter of agreement from the president included the following:

As vice president, you will be responsible for restructuring the units reporting to you. . . . It is critical that a new organization and culture be established during your tenure as vice president. . . . Consistent with our recent conversation, you will retire on or before December 31, 2014. We will begin a national search for your successor no later than July 1, 2013. Should the next vice president be in place before your retirement date, you will serve as senior advisor to the vice president.

As a result of our decision to pull most of the responsibilities for facilities into a single organization, the following units joined what was previously known as the Physical Plant division: Campus Park and Planning (maintains the campus

FRIB (Facility for Rare Isotope Beams) under construction. The enormous underground chamber required a 65-foot excavation in certain areas.

PHOTO COURTESY OF MSU COMMUNICATIONS AND BRAND STRATEGY.

master plan and ordinances, and manages Beal Gardens), Land Management (purchases and leases property, provides oversight of the farm district and the 20,000 acres away from East Lansing), Sustainability (provides leadership and develops strategies for MSU to be as environmentally "green" as possible), and Surplus Store and Recycling Center (disposes of unneeded items and expands campus recycling efforts). In addition, FRIB (Civil Infrastructure) would continue to report to my office.

As we moved into 2013, the organization's name would be changed to Infrastructure Planning and Facilities (IPF).

■ ■ ■

Vennie Gore proposed transferring the interior designers serving academic and athletic projects to IPF. This was a major step in providing campus customers with "one-stop shopping." (In the early 1960s an interior designer was hired into Housing and Food Services because it was acknowledged that housing units needed to be kept attractive for the student occupants. But no unnecessary money was to be spent on interior décor in any other campus buildings.)

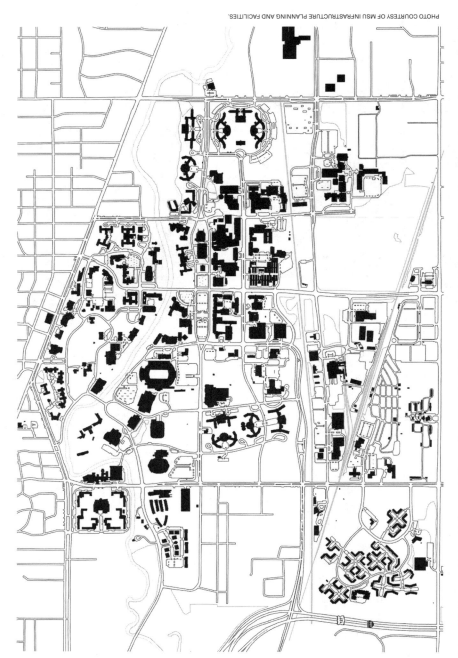

A current campus map, which reveals the major expansion that has occurred in the past 60 years. An enlarged current campus map is available at *http://maps.msu.edu.*

We created the new position of director of Engineering and Architectural Services and selected Dan Bollman for the role.

The most significant construction project during 2013 was the new fueling station and car wash built on Service Road. (When MSU was reviewed by the Homeland Security team, they noted that the old fueling station, under the east side of the stadium, with large gasoline and diesel fuel tanks buried nearby, was the greatest hazard on campus.)

On December 13, 2013, the Board of Trustees announced that Kemel Dawkins, from Rutgers University, would replace me as vice president for IPF, effective January 1, 2014.

■   ■   ■

A great accomplishment took place on January 1, 2014: The MSU Spartans football team won the Rose Bowl. This was personally rewarding, as I had developed a standard response to the frequently asked question, "When are you going to retire?" After all, I had continued to work well beyond the normal retirement age of 65. My response was, "Sometime after the next Rose Bowl victory." Our last Rose Bowl victory had been in 1988.

A few years earlier, Al Granger of Granger Construction was provoking me about retirement, and, after getting my classic response, he laughed and started to walk away. Then he turned back and said, "Ron, I'm not sure I can live that long!"

During 2014, the $24.5 million North End Zone Addition to Spartan Stadium was finished. One can only hope that the east side of the stadium will receive a similar renovation in the near future.

Also during 2014, the renovation to Akers Hall dining facilities, The Edge, completed the eight dining hall makeovers started in 2005, which had required an investment exceeding $300 million. Construction also began on the $60.8 million Bio Engineering facility that connects to both the Life Sciences building and the Clinical Center.

■   ■   ■

Kemel Dawkins had initially intended to move from Philadelphia, Pennsylvania, to Michigan, but numerous family issues required that he keep his family in Philadelphia and commute to his job at MSU. By the fall of 2014, he realized he could not be successful as the vice president while continuing to commute. He resigned his position at MSU and returned to Pennsylvania to pursue other opportunities.

MSU decided Dan Bollman should step up and become the new IPF leader. I believe this was a wise move. Dan has the depth, desire, and determination required for success in this role.

■   ■   ■

As I write these concluding thoughts, it is clear that "the concrete *still* never sets on John Hannah's campus." (For some of us, it will *always* be John Hannah's campus.) A $156 million housing and mixed-use development (1855 Place) is underway at the site of the old Michigan State Police headquarters, west of Harrison Road, and across the street from the Breslin Student Events Center, which is receiving a $50 million renovation. Also, an $88 million Research Center for the College of Human Medicine is currently under construction in Grand Rapids.

AFTERWORD

While researching the history of the MSU lanterns that were on the Farm Lane Bridge during the early 1950s, I discovered that the current concrete bridge was a New Deal Public Works Administration (PWA) project. (PWA projects, begun in 1933, were designed to put people to work and help move the nation out of the Great Depression.) Additionally, I discovered the PWA also provided funding for several buildings at what was then Michigan State College: Mason-Abbot Halls, the Veterinary addition to Giltner Hall, the Livestock Judging Pavilion (removed in 1997), Campbell Hall, Olin Health Center (first phase), the Auditorium, Jenison Fieldhouse, the Music building, and the addition to the North Campus Power Plant (removed in 1966).

These buildings were built between 1938 and 1940 and significantly expanded the square footage of permanent facilities at this small agricultural college with only 6,000 students.

All of this campus expansion took place less than 20 years before my arrival.

■   ■   ■

Having worked for nine of the 20 MSU presidents, I frequently get asked who I think had the greatest impact. The above-mentioned growth, plus the great campus expansion of the 1960s, helps to place John Hannah at the top. However, the past 10 years have provided significant expansion to MSU's image and facilities, and that is due to the work of President Simon.

The following comments on President Simon's tenure recently appeared in the local newspaper:

> "She really has transformed [MSU] from kind of a sleepy mid-level Big Ten college to pushing the very best," said David Hollister, a former Lansing mayor and president of Prima Civitas, a community development nonprofit Simon helped create.
>
> In the process, she helped take MSU from a force in the regional economy to a player in the state economy.
>
> Those who know her say Simon understands the university's role not only as educational institution, but as economic engine for the state of Michigan.
>
> "When all is said and done, Lou Anna's tenure will equal—or maybe even exceed—John Hannah's." (*Lansing State Journal*, February 8, 2015)

I believe Hollister's assessment has merit.

Because of that—because MSU is constantly expanding, always changing—it's hard to imagine what this great university will look like in another 60 to 80 years. Yet I have no doubt that the faculty, staff, and administrators will continue to ensure that this is a world-class institution for research, education, and the shaping of lives. It has certainly shaped mine.

While I won't be around to see the results myself, I have every belief that the long legacy of excellence at MSU—the legacy that drew me here as a student and kept me here for an additional 55 years—will only continue to grow.

INDEX